THE BOOK OF WORSHIP

THE BOOK OF WORSHIP

compiled by

JOHN RANDALL
DENNIS

BETHANYHOUSE
Minneapolis, Minnesota

The Book of Worship
Copyright © 2007
John Randall Dennis

Cover design by Zandrah Kurland
Interior design by Melinda Schumacher

Note: Where hymns are quoted, the music composer appears at the top, under the title, and the author of the lyrics appears at the bottom, after last stanza.

Unless otherwise identified, Scripture quotations are from the HOLY BIBLE, NEW AMERICAN STANDARD BIBLE®, © Copyright The Lockman Foundation 1960, 1962, 1963, 1968, 1971, 1972, 1973, 1975, 1977, 1995. Used by permission. (www.lockman.org)

Scripture quotations identified The Message are from The Message. Copyright © 1993, 1994, 1995 by Eugene H. Peterson. Used by permission of NavPress Publishing Group.

Published by Bethany House Publishers
11400 Hampshire Avenue South
Bloomington, Minnesota 55438

Bethany House Publishers is a division of
Baker Publishing Group, Grand Rapids, Michigan.

Printed in the United States of America

ISBN-13: 978-0-7642-0067-0
ISBN-10: 0-7642-0067-4

Library of Congress Cataloging-in-Publication Data

Dennis, John Randall.
 The book of worship : 365 inspiring readings based on worship songs
and classic hymns / John Randall Dennis.
   p. cm.
 Summary: "An interdenominational worship devotional based on old and new hymns and songs. Includes Scripture, readings, and songs, with melody, for 365 days, thematically based on the Christian calendar"—Provided by publisher.
 Includes bibliographical references and index.
 ISBN-13: 978-0-7642-0067-0 (hardcover : alk. paper)
 ISBN-10: 0-7642-0067-4 (hardcover : alk. paper)
 1. Devotional calendars. 2. Hymns. 3. Sacred vocal music. I. Title.

 BV4811.D46 2007
 242'.3—dc22   2006027940

A c k n o w l e d g m e n t s

Let me take a moment to thank many friends, authors, songwriters, and publishers who have been vital to the development of this project.

First, thanks to my wife, Brenda, who sparked the initial idea of this project. For years I watched her assemble a worship companion to her Bible—a hymnal stuffed with praise chorus lyric sheets. Finally it dawned on me that her need for a personal worship resource was not unique. It caused me to ponder what elements of personal worship we all could use and which most of us generally do not have memorized.

I am deeply thankful for the Bethany House family—Kyle Duncan, Jeanne Hedrick, and Steve Oates—who embraced my vision for this project early on and overcame with me many logistical obstacles to see it become a reality. Further, the graphic artists of Bethany House have enlarged my vision to take this book much further than I ever imagined. I am deeply grateful to them for dedicating their gifts to this project.

For each Sunday, I have borrowed from *The Book of Common Prayer* by Thomas Cranmer, trying to modify the approach to be useful to contemporary Christians. I've also edited his text, originally penned in the 1500s, to make his prayers more understandable and accessible.

Additionally, I gratefully acknowledge the following publishers for generously permitting me to quote brief excerpts. I heartily recommend that you read these sources to fully appreciate these excellent authors:

Breaking Free by Beth Moore,
    Broadman & Holman Publishers, Nashville, TN, 2000
Believing God by Beth Moore,
    Broadman & Holman Publishers, Nashville, TN, 2001
Hope for Each Day by Billy Graham,
    Thomas Nelson, Nashville, TN, 2002
A Glimpse of Jesus by Brennan Manning,
    HarperSanFrancisco, New York, NY, 2003
Various writings by C. S. Lewis,
    published by Macmillan Publishing Co., Inc., London
Poems by C. S. Lewis,
    Harvest Books/Harcourt, San Diego, CA, 2002
Letters From the Desert by Carlo Carretto,
    Orbis Books, Maryknoll, NY, 1974
The Miracle of Life Change by Chip Ingram,
    Zondervan, Grand Rapids, MI, 2000
The Hiding Place by Corrie ten Boom,
    Chosen Books, Chappaqua, NY, 1984
A Pilgrim's Almanac by Edward Hayes,
    Ave Maria Press, Notre Dame, IN, 1989
Seizing Your Divine Moment by Erwin Raphael McManus,
    Thomas Nelson, Nashville, TN, 2002
The Message by Eugene Peterson,
    NavPress, Colorado Springs, CO, 1993
The Complete Works of Francis A. Schaeffer by Francis Schaeffer,
    Crossway Books, Westchester, IL,1982
Be Still and Know by Georgia Harkness,
    Abingdon Press, Nashville, TN, 1953
Optimism by Helen Keller,
    Kessinger Publishing, Whitefish, MT, 2003

The Lord is Near by Mark Neilsen,
 Creative Communications for the Parish, 1993
"Advent Prayer" by Henri J. M. Nouwen,
 Henri Nouwen Society, New York, NY, n.d.
A Cry for Mercy by Henri J. M. Nouwen,
 Image/Doubleday, New York, NY, 1983
A Treasury of Christmas Stories by Henry Van Dyke,
 Harold Shaw Publishers, Colorado Springs, CO, 1993
Surprised by the Voice of God by Jack Deere,
 Zondervan, Grand Rapids, MI, 1998
Waking the Dead by John Eldridge,
 Thomas Nelson, Nashville, TN, 2003
Taste and See by John Piper,
 Multnomah, Sisters, OR, 2005
He Who Began a Good Work by Jon Mohr,
 Birdwing Music, Nashville, TN, 1988
Light Came at Christmas by Karen L. Oberst, 2001,
 with permission of the author
"Jesus the Healer" from a sermon by Kathryn Kuhlman,
 The Kathryn Kuhlman Foundation, Pittsburgh, PA, 1965
The Glorious Impossible by Madeleine L'Engle,
 Simon & Schuster, New York, NY, 1990
Penguins and Golden Calves by Madeleine L'Engle,
 Harold Shaw Publishers, Colorado Springs, CO, 2003
Walking on Water by Madeleine L'Engle,
 Harold Shaw Publishers, Colorado Springs, CO, 2001
The Ordering of Love by Madeleine L'Engle,
 Harold Shaw Publishers, Colorado Springs, CO, 2005
God Is Your Hope by Marie Shropshire,
 Harvest House Publishers, 2001
He Still Moves Stones by Max Lucado,
 W Publishing Group, Nashville, TN, 1993

Let the Journey Begin by Max Lucado,
    W Publishing Group, Nashville, TN, 1998
The Workbook on Lessons From the Saints by Maxie Dunnam,
    The Upper Room, Nashville, TN, 2002
Violent Grace by Michael Card,
    Mole End Music (admin. by Word Music), Nashville, TN, 2000
A Treasury of Wisdom by Mrs. Charles E. Cowman,
    Zondervan, Grand Rapids, MI, 1925
Strength for the Storm by Richard Exley,
    Thomas Nelson, Nashville, TN, 1999
The Purpose-Driven Life by Rick Warren,
    Zondervan, Grand Rapids, MI, 2002
The Book of Family Prayer by Robert Webber,
    Hendrickson Publishers, Peabody, MA,1986
A Guide to Prayer for Ministers and Other Servants
    by Ruben P. Job & Norman Shawchuck,
    The Upper Room, Nashville, TN, 1983
Smith Wigglesworth: The Complete Collection of His Life
    by Roberts Liardon, Harrison House, Tulsa, OK, 1997
A Faith for All Seasons by Ted M. Dorman,
    Broadman & Holman, Nashville, TN, 1995
Preparing for Jesus by Walter Wangerin Jr.,
    Zondervan, Grand Rapids, MI, 2005

Also, many thanks to Debra Mayes of Integrity Music (Mobile, Alabama),
a great friend who has graciously allowed us to use several of their out-
standing worship songs:

"Open the Eyes of My Heart" by Paul Baloche
"Shout to the Lord" by Darlene Zschech
"Above All" by Paul Baloche
"Trading My Sorrows" by Darrell Evans

"I Give You My Heart" by Reuben Morgan
"Give Thanks" by Henry Smith
"My Redeemer Lives" by Reuben Morgan
"Ancient of Days" by Jamie Harvill and Gary Sadler
"More Precious Than Silver" by Lynn DeShazo
"I Worship You, Almighty God" by Sondra Corbett
"The Potter's Hand" by Darlene Zschech
"Everyday" by Joel Houston
"Jesus, Name Above All Names" by Naida Hearn
"You Are Good" by Israel Houghton
"There Is None Like You" by Lenny LeBlanc
"Mighty Is Our God" by Eugene Greco, Gerrit Gustafson, and Don Moen
"Blessed Be the Lord God Almighty" by Bob Fitts
"Come Into His Presence" by Lynne Baird
"Rise Up and Praise Him" by Paul Baloche and Gary Sadler
"Worthy, You Are Worthy" by Don Moen
"Think About His Love" by Walt Harrah
"When I Look Into Your Holiness" by Wayne and Cathy Perrin
"Praise Adonai" by Paul Baloche
"Holy Spirit, Rain Down" by Russell Fragar
"Let There Be Glory and Honor and Praises"
        by James and Elizabeth Greenelsh
"Before the Throne of God Above" by Vikki Cook and Charitie Lees Bancroft
"Your Love Is Extravagant" by Darrell Evans
"We All Bow Down" by Lenny LeBlanc
"Be Exalted, O God" by Brent Chambers
"Lord, Have Mercy" by Steve Merkel
"Still" by Reuben Morgan
"You Are Near" by Reuben Morgan
"To Him Who Sits on the Throne" by Debbye Graafsma
"Only by Grace" by Gerrit Gustafson
"How Great Are You, Lord" by Lynn DeShazo

Finally, let me thank Bill and Jeanette Manchester, who have labored with me in the development of scores, researching sources from my scratchy recollections and notes, and securing permissions. I simply could not have completed this work without them.

I do hope this tool crosses historical and theological boundaries to embrace in unity what we all agree on: Our loving Father is worthy of worship. We hold Jesus and His finished work for us precious. We embrace the care, fellowship, and person of the Spirit. Praise to all Three!

Table of Contents

INTRODUCTION

Our lives are made up of cycles and seasons. Of course, we walk through a linear succession of events and relationships. But underneath all the components of birth, childhood, education, friendships, marriage, joys, hardships, jobs, parenting... there's a rhythm. It's as if God has orchestrated the music of our lives to a time signature, counting 1-2-3-4, 1-2-3-4... morning, noonday, evening, night, Sunday through Saturday, January through December, 1-2-3-4.

> *"Summer and winter and springtime and harvest,*
> *Sun, moon, and stars in their courses above*
> *Join with all nature in manifest witness*
> *To thy great faithfulness, mercy, and love."*

God made the entire cosmos work this way. It was His idea. And these rhythms testify to His greatness just as surely as the skies proclaim the works of His hands. For Israel, He instituted a yearly cycle of holy days. His people labored, rested, feasted, lit candles, read the Torah, prayed, blessed. These days were not only observed in obedience, they were also opportunities to teach the young and remind themselves of God's goodness.

Though they were not compelled by God's law, the early church recognized this rhythm too. They seized the opportunity to use cycles and seasons to frame and reinforce oral teachings about God,

Christ, the Holy Spirit, and the church. Their calendar was built of components ensuring Christians were taught "Christianity 101" and celebrated God's faithfulness, mercy, and love. These components (appearing in bold) include the following.

Advent recognizes how the world yearns for and needs Jesus. It establishes His divinity as God's only begotten Son. Christmas celebrates what Madeleine L'Engle calls "the glorious impossible"—the exalted King of angels humbly clothing himself in flesh. Epiphany deals with the world's early recognition of Him in ordinary circumstances—Magi recognizing the King through the revelation in nature, rabbis recognizing His spiritual authority through the revelation of His teaching, and His own cousin recognizing He was the Anointed One, the Lamb of God. Lent, Holy Week, and Easter teach His intentionality and depth of passion for us. Pentecost tells of the arrival and power of the promised Comforter. It celebrates the church age, the age of the Holy Spirit. The Season After Pentecost points to our lives in the Spirit, the gifts of the Spirit, and the ever-increasing kingdom of heaven on earth. Then, because we need to be reminded and given the opportunity to see these things in deeper, richer levels, it starts all over again. 1-2-3-4, 1-2-3-4...

The calendar was one of several tools the church later used to instruct a largely oral society in which not everyone had Bibles. Church building floor plans were shaped like crosses, and they soared in height to express God's magnificence. Music was written in particular, symbolic ways. Windows carefully brought in light to lift the spirit. Stained glass was crafted not as abstract artistic expressions but as portrayals of specific Bible stories, creating opportunities to teach and learn. This all was the multimedia of their time.

You and I need tools like this too, even in the hectic, electronic Information Age. Maybe even more than ever! If you're like me, life is often busy and distracting. This underlying rhythmic cycle helps me stay in balance. It pulls me from merely focusing on needs in my life's sequential events and returns my eyes to an ever-beneficent God, a beautiful Savior, an embracing Spirit.

The Book of Worship is one of these tools. I conceived it as a Bible companion for worship, whether personal or in groups. It's meant to offer rhythm and structure without confinement. Here are some of its benefits:

P r a y e r s   a n d   R e a d i n g s

There are enough prayers and readings for each day. They're organized loosely around the Christian calendar cycle. So if you want to use one per day for your worship, you can. And it will be appropriate to the time of year you use it. But *The Book of Worship* isn't so rigidly structured that if you aren't able to use these every day, you'll get behind. To miss a few readings doesn't mean you have "fallen off the cart." Just go to the section appropriate for the season and pick any day's reading. The book is purposely designed to be available when you need it—daily or periodically.

These prayers and readings are by Christians from all traditions and all ages; they come from people well known, less known, and unknown. I like that because there is so much rich and good material to be enjoyed that is offered by contemporary Christians, Christians from ages past, and those from every time in between. It doesn't matter whether you're a traditionalist or a seeker, a denominationalist or an independent—there is so much we agree on when we focus on worshiping Jesus. And the rich diversity found here is healthy because it enables us to stretch and see Him the way someone else enjoys Him.

H y m n s   a n d   S o n g s

There are enough well-known hymns and songs for about three weekly. I've tried to identify the best-known hymns and choruses, the ones people continually sing or need in particular seasons. Every hymn and song lyric I enjoy is rooted in Scripture—whether as a direct quotation or by allusion. These verses are referenced as footnotes with each lyric. You can dwell on a song for a while, see where the lyric idea came from, and go directly to the Bible to deepen and extend its message.

L a n g u a g e

I think there's merit in hearing these prayers, hymns, and songs as they were originally written. The only paraphrasing I've done was to elements where language so got in the way as to obscure the message. Sometimes readings written in the 1600s are easily understood in the twenty-first century; sometimes they're not. If easily understood, I left the language as originally written. On rare occasions there's a word in a lyric or reading whose definition has been lost. In those instances I either footnoted the definition or changed the word.

In *The Book of Worship* I have tried to offer you rich and meaningful worship tools...in the context of great freedom. It's meant to enrich and augment, not constrict your worship. It's meant to help you in worship when you're away from a structured public setting.

Moreover, it's intended to help you know God and enjoy Him. He knows and enjoys you. And as you get to know Him better, you'll find He's not far off at all. He's not as religious as you may think. One of my friends said it so well: "We don't worship God to get His attention. We worship Him because we have His attention!"

Abba, You are so eager to spend time with me.
I don't need to beg You to come. You have come!
Thank you!
Help me to really meet You—
    not always as the god I expect, but as the God You are.
Please reveal Yourself right now in ways I can understand,
    then enlarge my understanding.
Help me to trust You enough to let go of my heart and my head
    so I can be renewed.
We really do love You,
    and we want to know You more...so we can have
    more to love.
Amen.

PREFACE

All our lives we hunger for You...even when we don't truly comprehend the nature of our hunger. Vainly we search for substitutions that pale in comparison to You. We fill our days with distractions to avoid the sound of our spirits' heaving sighs, longing for You. What futility! Our souls will never find their rest until they rest in Your arms.

Today, this moment, this year—we turn our gaze to Your stunning beauty. We listen for Your voice, for Your mouth is full of sweetness. We breathe in the fragrance of life, the very scent of You. We long for Your touch in our inmost places and seek to lay our heads lovingly on Your breast. We want to taste and see how good You really are.

Holy Spirit, reveal the true nature of our heavenly Father through Jesus the Christ. Today, this moment, this year—show Yourself with power. And when You are revealed we will laugh and dance and tremble and weep. We will discover Your peace.

We worship You.

ADVENT

This is a season of remembering how greatly *we needed You. How dark and heavy was our bitter captivity. How bright these days of breathing free air! We recall the bittersweet longing. The slavery. Tears. Long, empty nights.*

But You came in the flesh. You came to unlock our chains.

You come as the bona fide King of the Universe, disguised as a child. You establish Your kingdom among the unlikely. You make mere mortals Your friends, knighting them as princes and princesses. You celebrate life with even the ugliest and the outcast. You ask, "What can I do for you?" You exude such great kindness that it leads us to change the very course of our lives and how we live.

This is a season of sadness past. This is a season anticipating joys to come. Our spirits burn with excited expectation. Maranatha!

FIRST SUNDAY OF ADVENT

Almighty God, give us grace to cast away works of darkness and to put on armour of light, now in the time of this mortal life, in which your Son Jesus Christ came to us in great humility; that on the last day, when He comes again in His glorious majesty to judge the living and the dead, we may rise to the life immortal; through Him who is alive and reigns with You, in the unity of the Spirit, one God, now and for ever.

—THOMAS CRANMER, 1489–1556

INCARNATION

The Son of God became a man to enable men to become sons of God.

—C. S. LEWIS, 1898–1963

COME, THOU LONG-EXPECTED JESUS

—ROWLAND H. PRICHARD, 1830

Come, Thou long - ex - pect - ed Je - sus Born to set Thy peo - ple free.[1]

From our fears and sins re - lease[2] us; Let us find our rest in Thee.

Is - rael's Strength and Con - so - la - tion[3] Hope of all the earth Thou art -

Dear De - sire of ev - 'ry na - tion,[4] Joy of ev - 'ry - long - ing heart!

2. Born Thy people to deliver,[5]
born a child, and yet a king,
born to reign in us for ever,
now Thy gracious kingdom[6] bring.
By Thine own eternal Spirit
rule in all our hearts alone;
by Thine all-sufficient merit
raise us to Thy glorious throne.

1. Isaiah 61:1
2. Luke 4:18
3. Luke 2:25
4. Haggai 2:7
5. Daniel 12:1
6. Isaiah 9:7
Also Acts 13:32-33

—CHARLES WESLEY, 1744

4

WONDER AND HUNGER

Come, long-expected Jesus. Excite in me a wonder at the wisdom and power of Your Father and ours. Receive my prayer as part of my service of the Lord who enlists me in God's own work for justice.

Come, long-expected Jesus. Excite in me a hunger for peace: peace in the world, peace in my home, peace in myself.

—UNKNOWN

THIS IS THE MONTH

This is the month, and this the happy morn,
Wherein the Son of Heaven's Eternal King,
Of wedded maid and virgin mother born,
Our great redemption from above did bring;
For so the holy sages once did sing,
That He our deadly forfeit should release,
And with His Father work us a perpetual peace.

—JOHN MILTON, 1608–1674

JOY AND LOVE AND PEACE

Come, long-expected Jesus. Excite in me a joy responsive to the Father's joy. I seek His will so I can serve with gladness, singing, and love.

Come, long-expected Jesus. Excite in me the joy and love and peace it is right to bring to the manger of my Lord. Raise in me, too, sober reverence for the God who acted there, hearty gratitude for the life begun there, and spirited resolution to serve the Father and Son.

I pray in the name of Jesus Christ, whose advent I hail. Amen.

—UNKNOWN

GOD'S GOODNESS

God's goodness hath been great to thee;
Let never day or night unhallowed pass,
But still remember what the Lord hath done.

—WILLIAM SHAKESPEARE, 1564–1616

ADVENT FIRE

Fire is a fitting sign to help us celebrate Advent.... If Christ is to come more fully into our lives this Christmas, if God is to become really incarnate for us, then fire will have to be present in our prayer. Our worship and devotion will have to stoke the kind of fire in our souls that can truly change our hearts. Ours is a great responsibility not to waste this Advent time.

—EDWARD HAYES, *A Pilgrim's Almanac*, 1989

O COME, O COME, EMMANUEL

−PLAINSONG, 15TH CENTURY

O Come, O come Em - man - u - el, and ran-som[1] cap tive Is - ra - el, that

mourns in lone-ly ex - ile here un - til the Son of God ap - pear.

Refrain

Re - joice! Re - joice! Em - man - u - el[2] shall come to Thee, O Is - ra - el.

2. O come, thou Wisdom from on high,
Who orderest all things mightily;
to us the path of knowledge show,
and teach us in her ways to go.
> *Refrain*

3. O come, thou Rod of Jesse,[3] free
Thine own from Satan's tyranny;
from depths of hell Thy people save,
and give them victory o'er the grave.
> *Refrain*

4. O come, Thou Dayspring,[4] come
and cheer
our spirits by Thine advent here;
disperse the gloomy clouds of night,
and death's dark shadows put to
flight.
> *Refrain*

5. O come, Thou Root of Jesse's[5] tree,
an ensign of Thy people be;
before Thee rulers silent fall;
all peoples on Thy mercy call.
> *Refrain*

6. O come, Desire of nations,[6] bind
in one the hearts of all mankind;
bid Thou our sad divisions cease,
and be Thyself our King of Peace.
> *Refrain*

1. Isaiah 51:11
2. Isaiah 7:14
3. Psalm 2:9
4. Luke 1:78
5. Isaiah 11:10
6. Haggai 2:7

−LATIN, 9TH CENTURY

7

SECOND SUNDAY OF ADVENT

O Lord, raise up, we pray, Your power
and come among us,
and with great might succour us;
that whereas, through our sins and wickedness
we are grievously hindered
in running the race that is set before us,
Your bountiful grace and mercy
may speedily help and deliver us;
through Jesus Christ Your Son our Lord,
to whom with You and the Holy Spirit,
be honour and glory, now and for ever.

—THOMAS CRANMER, 1489–1556

GLORIOUS IMPOSSIBLES

Possible things are easy to believe. The Glorious Impossibles are what bring joy to our hearts, hope to our lives, songs on our lips.

—MADELEINE L'ENGLE, 1918-

CHRIST, REDEEMER OF ALL PERSONS

Christ, redeemer of all persons,
from the Father, His only begotten,
Alone before the beginning
born without being made.

You are the light, the Father's splendour,
You are the everlasting hope of all persons,
accept, how prayers flow throughout
the world from Your begotten.

Remember, Author of salvation,
how being born of a chaste virgin
You have assumed the form
of our self-same body.

So does today testify, and throughout
the orbit of years, that You are
the sole Advent from the Father's
throne for the world's salvation.

—AMBROSE, C. 339–397

LO! HOW A ROSE E'ER BLOOMING

—German, 15th century

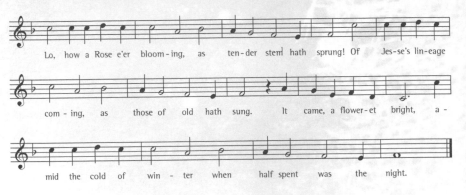

Lo, how a Rose e'er bloom-ing, as ten-der stem hath sprung! Of Jes-se's lin-eage

com - ing, as those of old hath sung. It came, a flower-et bright, a -

mid the cold of win - ter when half spent was the night.

2. Isaiah[2] 'twas foretold it,
   the Rose I have in mind;
   With Mary we behold it,
   the virgin[3] mother kind.
   To show God's love aright,
   she bore to us a Savior,
   When half spent was the night.

3. This Flower, whose fragrance tender
   with sweetness fills the air,
   Dispels with glorious splendor
   the darkness everywhere;
   True Man, yet very God,
   from sin and death He saves us,
   And lightens every load.

4. O Savior, Child of Mary,
   Who felt our human woe,
   O Savior, King of glory,
   Who dost our weakness know[4];
   Bring us at length we pray,
   to the bright courts of heaven,
   And to the endless day.

1. Isaiah 11:1
2. Isaiah 53:2
3. Isaiah 7:14
4. Hebrews 4:15
Also Song of Solomon 2:1

—German, 15th century

THIS NEW HYMN

Be it this heaven, this earth,
be it this sea and all these contain,
that they praise lifting their chant
to the Author of your coming forth.

And even we, redeemed
with Your holy blood,
on this Your christmasday,
sing together this new hymn:

Glory be to you, o Lord,
who was of a virgin born,
with Father and Holy Spirit
for all ages everlasting.

—AMBROSE, C. 339–397

COMFORT, COMFORT YE MY PEOPLE

Comfort, comfort ye my people,
speak ye peace, thus saith our God;
comfort those who sit in darkness,
mourning 'neath their sorrow's load;
speak ye to Jerusalem
of the peace that waits for them;
tell her that her sins I cover,
and her warfare now is over.

—JOHANN G. OLEARIUS, 1611–1684

THY KINGDOM COME, O GOD

Thy kingdom come, O God!
Thy rule, O Christ begin!
Break with Thine iron rod
the tyrannies of sin!

—LEWIS HENSLEY, 1824–1905

THERE'S A VOICE IN THE WILDERNESS

There's a voice in the wilderness crying,
A call from the ways untrod:
Prepare in the desert a highway,
A highway for our God!
The valleys shall be exalted,
The lofty hills brought low;
Make straight all the crooked places,
Where the Lord our God may go!

—JAMES L. MILLIGAN, 1876–1961

THIRD SUNDAY OF ADVENT

O Lord Jesus Christ,
At Your first coming You sent Your messenger
to prepare Your way before You:
Grant that the ministers and stewards of Your mysteries
may likewise so prepare and make ready Your way
by turning the hearts of the disobedient
to the wisdom of the just,
that at Your second coming to judge the world
we may be found an acceptable people in Your sight;
for you are alive and reign with the Father
in the unity of the Holy Spirit,
one God, now and for ever. Amen.

—THOMAS CRANMER, 1489–1556

LET ALL MORTAL FLESH KEEP SILENCE

FRENCH, 17TH CENTURY

Let all mor-tal flesh keep si - lence[1] and with fear and tremb - ling[2] stand;

pon - der noth-ing earth - ly mind - ed, for with bless-ing in his hand;

Christ our God to earth de - scend - eth our full hom-age to de - mand.

2. King of kings, yet born of Mary,
   As of old on earth He stood,
   Lord of lords, in human vesture,
   In the body and the blood;
   He will give to all the faithful
   His own self for heavenly food.

3. Rank on rank the host of heaven
   Spreads its vanguard on the way,
   As the Light of light descendeth[3]
   From the realms of endless day,
   That the powers of hell may vanish
   As the darkness clears away.

4. At His feet the six-wingèd seraph,[4]
   Cherubim with sleepless eye,
   Veil their faces to the presence,
   As with ceaseless voice they cry:
   Alleluia, Alleluia,
   Alleluia, Lord Most High.

1. Habakkuk 2:20
2. Philippians 2:12
3. John 1:56
4. Isaiah 6:2

—LITURGY OF ST. JAMES

EARTH WAS WAITING

Earth was waiting, spent and restless,
with a mingled hope and fear,
faithful men and women praying,
"Surely, Lord, the day is near:
the Desire of all the nations—
it is time He should appear!"

Then the Spirit of the Highest
to a Virgin meek came down,
and He burdened Her with blessing,
and He pained her with renown;
for she bore the Lord's Anointed
for His cross and for His crown.

—WALTER CHALMERS SMITH, 1824–1908

ALL THROUGH THIS DAY

*All through this day, O Lord, by the power of Thy quickening Spirit,
let me touch the lives of others for good, whether through the word
I speak, the prayer I speak, or the life I live.*

—ANONYMOUS

THE ADVENT OF OUR GOD

The advent of our God
with eager prayers we greet,
and singing haste upon His road
His glorious gift to meet.

The everlasting Son
scorns not a Virgin's womb;
that we from bondage may be won
He bears a bondsman's doom.

Daughter of Zion, rise
to meet thy lowly King,
let not thy stubborn heart despise
the peace He deigns to bring.

—CHARLES COFFIN, 1676–1749

COME EVEN NOW

O Lord, stir up, we beg you, your power—and come. Come even now into this season of our meditations, that by your protection we may be rescued from our sins, and saved by your mighty deliverance in order to look forward to your final arrival with the joy that cannot be uttered. We pray in your name, O Lord, for you live and reign with the Father and the Holy Spirit, one God, now and forever. Amen.

—WALTER WANGERIN JR. 1944–

OF THE FATHER'S LOVE BEGOTTEN

—Plainsong, 16th century

Of the Fa-ther's love be-got - ten, Ere the worlds be-gan to be, He is Al-pha and O-me - ga

He the Source, the End - ing He, Of the things that are, that have been,

And that fu - ture years shall see Ev - er-more and ev - er-more a - men.

2. At His Word the worlds were framèd;
   He commanded; it was done:
   Heaven and earth and depths of ocean
   in their threefold order one;
   All that grows beneath the shining
   Of the moon and burning sun,
   evermore and evermore!

3. He is found in human fashion,
   death and sorrow here to know,
   That the race of Adam's children
   doomed by law to endless woe,
   May not henceforth die and perish
   In the dreadful gulf below,
   evermore and evermore!

4. O that birth forever blessèd,
   when the virgin, full of grace,
   By the Holy Ghost conceiving,

bare the Savior of our race;
And the Babe, the world's Redeemer,
First revealed His sacred face,
evermore and evermore!

5. O ye heights of heaven adore Him;
   angel hosts, His praises sing;
   Powers, dominions, bow before Him,
   and extol our God and King!
   Let no tongue on earth be silent,
   Every voice in concert sing,
   evermore and evermore!

6. Christ, to Thee with God the Father,
   and, O Holy Ghost, to Thee,
   Hymn and chant with high thanksgiving,
   and unwearied praises be:
   Honor, glory, and dominion,
   And eternal victory,[3]
   evermore and evermore!

1. John 1:14-18
2. Revelation 1:8
3. 1 Corinthians 15:57
Also Revelation 22:13

—A.C. PRUDENTIUS, 5TH CENTURY

YOUR BEAUTIFUL NATURE

How long we listen'd for Your approaching steps.
For years, our eyes scanned the horizon for Your coming.
We had anticipated the spectacle of a conquering sovereign.
We looked for flowing robes, gleaming gold in the sun—
    not a baby born in a cave, wrapped in rags.
Yet You came not to conquer, but to serve...
    not to judge, but to love the undeserving.
Such is Your beautiful nature.

—JOHN RANDALL DENNIS, 1957-

THAT GLORIOUS FORM

That glorious Form, that Light unsufferable,
And that far-beaming blaze of Majesty
Wherewith He wont at Heaven's high council
To sit the midst of Triunal Unity.
He laid aside; and, here with us to be,
Forsook the courts of everlasting day,
And chose with us a darksome house of mortal clay.

—JOHN MILTON, 1608–1674

FOURTH SUNDAY OF ADVENT

God our Redeemer, who prepared the blessed Virgin Mary to be the mother of your Son: grant that, as she looked for his coming as our Savior, so we will be ready to greet him when he comes again as our judge; who is alive and reigns with you, in the unity of the Holy Spirit, one God, now and for ever. Amen.

—THOMAS CRANMER, 1489–1556

EARTH HAS GROANED

Earth has groaned and labored for Him
since the ages first began,
for in Him was hid the secret
which through all the ages ran—
Son of Mary, Son of David,
Son of God, and Son of Man.

—WALTER CHALMERS SMITH, 1824–1908

ADVENT PRAYER

Master of both the light and the darkness,
*   send your Holy Spirit upon our preparations for Christmas.*
We who have so much to do seek quiet spaces
*   to hear your voice each day.*
We who are anxious over many things look forward
*   to your coming among us.*
We who are blessed in so many ways long for
*   the complete joy of your kingdom.*
We whose hearts are heavy seek the joy of your presence.
We are your people, walking in darkness, yet seeking the light.
To you we say, "Come Lord Jesus!"
Amen.

—MARK NEILSEN, 1948–

THE UNENDING MIRACLE

Truly, this is the unending miracle of love:
that one loving person, through his love, can embrace God,
Whose being fills and transcends the entire creation.

—ANONYMOUS, 14TH CENTURY

THE FIRE OF GOD

The fire of God, which is his essential being, his love, his creative
power, is a fire unlike its earthly symbol in this, that it is only at a
distance it burns—that the farther from him, it burns the worse, and
that when we turn and begin to approach him, the burning begins to
change to comfort, which comfort will grow to such bliss that the
heart at length cries out with a gladness no other gladness can reach,
"Whom have I in heaven but thee? and there is none upon earth that
I desire besides thee!"

—GEORGE MACDONALD, 1824–1905

THREE CANDLES, ONE LIGHT

Tell me how it is that in this room there are three candles and but
one light, and I will explain to you the mode of the divine existence.

—JOHN WESLEY, 1844–1908

BREAK FORTH, O BEAUTEOUS HEAVENLY LIGHT

—Johann Schop, 1641

Break forth, O beau-te-ous heaven-ly light, and ush-er in the morn-ing; O shep-herds, shrink not with a-fright[1] but hear the an-gel's warn-ing. This child, now weak in in-fan-cy,[2] our con-fi-dence and joy shall be, the power of Sa-tan break-ing,[3] our peace e-ter-nal mak-ing.

1. Luke 2:9-10
2. Isaiah 7:14
3. Ephesians 2:14
Also Luke 2:32

—Johann Rist, 1641

CHRISTMAS

Twelve days to celebrate Your nearness...to linger in the joy of what Your coming has meant to a lost world, to me. One day could not contain it.

Your coming heralded our salvation—not merely from eternal wrath, but from sin. You came as our Salvation, our Healing, our Deliverance.

You came to enemies and made them Your sons and daughters.

Astounding!

Is it any wonder we worship You?

A PRAYER FOR CHRISTMAS MORNING

The day of joy returns, Father in Heaven,
and crowns another year with peace and good will.

Help us rightly to remember the birth of Jesus,
that we may share in the song of the angels,
the gladness of the shepherds,
and the worship of the wisemen.

Close the doors of hate and open the doors of love
all over the world...

Let kindness come with every gift
and good desires with every greeting.

Deliver us from evil, by the blessing that Christ brings,
and teach us to be merry with clean hearts.

May the Christmas morning make us happy
to be thy children, and the Christmas evening
bring us to our bed with grateful thoughts,
forgiving and forgiven, for Jesus' sake.

Amen.

—HENRY VAN DYKE, 1852-1933

O COME, ALL YE FAITHFUL

—ENGLISH, 1751

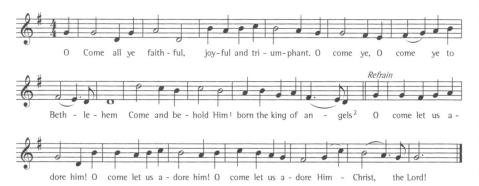

O Come all ye faith-ful, joy-ful and tri-um-phant. O come ye, O come ye to Beth - le - hem Come and be - hold Him¹ born the king of an - gels² O come let us a-dore him! O come let us a-dore him! O come let us a-dore Him - Christ, the Lord!

Refrain

2. True God of true God,
   Light from Light Eternal,
   Lo, He shuns not the Virgin's
       womb;
   Son of the Father, begotten,
   not created.
       Refrain

3. Sing, choirs of angels,
   sing in exultation;
   O sing, all ye citizens of
   heaven above!
   Glory to God, all
   glory in the highest!
       Refrain

4. Yea, Lord, we greet Thee,
   born this happy morning;
   Jesus, to Thee be all glory given;
   Word of the Father,
   now in flesh appearing.³
       Refrain

1. Luke 2:13-15
2. Hebrews 1:6
3. John 1:14

—LATIN, 18TH CENTURY

FIRST SUNDAY OF CHRISTMAS

Almighty God, who wonderfully created us in your own
image and yet more wonderfully restored us through your
Son Jesus Christ: grant that, as he came to share in our
humanity, we may share the life of his divinity; who is
alive and reigns with you, in the unity of the Spirit, one
God, now and for ever. Amen.

—THOMAS CRANMER, 1489–1556

SILENT NIGHT

—FRANZ GRÜBER, 1818

Si - lent night! ho - ly night! All is calm, all is bright Round yon vir - gin moth-er[1] and Child.

Ho-ly In-fant, so ten-der and mild Sleep in heav-en-ly peace Sleep in heav-en-ly peace.

2. Silent night! Holy night!
Shepherds quake at the sight;
Glories stream from heaven afar,
Heavenly hosts sing Alleluia![2]
Christ the Savior is born,
Christ the Savior is born!

3. Silent night! Holy night!
Son of God, love's pure light;
Radiant beams from Thy
    holy face
With the dawn of redeeming
    grace,
Jesus, Lord, at Thy birth,
Jesus, Lord, at Thy birth.

1. Matthew 1:23
2. Luke 2:13-16

—JOSEPH MOHR, 1818

27

GOOD CHRISTIAN MEN, REJOICE

—GERMAN, 14TH CENTURY

Good Christ - ian men re - joice with heart and soul and voice. Give ye heed to what we say: News! News! Je - sus Christ is born to - day!¹ Ox and ass be - fore Him bow, And He is in the man - ger now.² Christ is born to - day! Christ is born to - day!

2. Good Christian men, rejoice,
with heart and soul and voice;
Now ye hear of endless bliss:
Joy! Joy!
Jesus Christ was born for this!
He has opened the heavenly door,
and man is blest forevermore.
Christ was born for this!
Christ was born for this!

3. Good Christian men, rejoice,
with heart and soul and voice;
Now ye need not fear the grave:
Peace! Peace!
Jesus Christ was born to save.³
Calls you one and calls you all,
to gain His everlasting hall.
Christ was born to save!
Christ was born to save!

1. Luke 2:11
2. Luke 2:12
3. I Timothy 1:15
Also Matthew 2:10

—HEINRICH SUSO, n.d.; TRANS. JOHN M. NEALE, 1853

ANGELS WE HAVE HEARD ON HIGH

—FRENCH CAROL, 18TH CENTURY

An-gels we have heard on high[1] sweet-ly sing-ing o'er the plains, And the moun-tains in re-ply,

Ech-o-ing their joy-ous strains. Glo - - - - - - - ri - a.

Refrain

in ex-cel-sis De - o![2] Glo - - - - - - - ri - a

in ex - cel - sis De - o!

1. Luke 2:13
2. Luke 2:14
3. Luke 2:8
4. Luke 2:15
5. Luke 2:12

2. Shepherds, why this jubilee?[3]
   Why your joyous strains prolong?
   What the gladsome tidings be
   Which inspire your heavenly song?
   Refrain

3. Come to Bethlehem and see[4]
   Christ Whose birth the angels sing;
   Come, adore on bended knee,
   Christ the Lord, the newborn King.
   Refrain

4. See Him in a manger laid,[5]
   Whom the choirs of angels praise;
   Mary, Joseph, lend your aid,
   While our hearts in love we raise.
   Refrain

—FRENCH CAROL, 18TH CENTURY

CHRISTMAS BRINGETH JESUS

Earth, strike up your music,
Birds that sing and bells that ring;
Heaven hath answering music
For all Angels soon to sing:
Earth, put on your whitest
Bridal robe of spotless snow:
For Christmas bringeth Jesus,
Brought for us so low.

—CHRISTINA ROSSETTI, 1830–1894

A PRAYER FROM SPACE

Give us, O God, the vision which can see
Your love in the world in spite of human failure.
Give us the faith to trust Your goodness
in spite of our ignorance and weakness.
Give us the knowledge that we may continue to pray
with understanding hearts.
And show us what each one of us can do
to set forward the coming of the day of universal peace.

—FRANK BORMAN, FROM A MOON-ORBITING MISSION, DECEMBER 1968

AWAY IN A MANGER

—James Murray, 1887

A - way in a man-ger, no crib for a bed,[1] The lit - tle Lord Je - sus laid down His sweet head. The stars in the sky looked down where He lay, The lit - tle Lord Je - sus a - sleep on the hay.

2. The cattle are lowing, the Baby awakes,
   But little Lord Jesus, no crying He makes;
   I love Thee, Lord Jesus, look down from the sky
   And stay by my cradle, til morning is nigh.

3. Be near me, Lord Jesus, I ask Thee to stay
   Close by me forever, and love me, I pray;
   Bless all the dear children in Thy tender care,
   And fit us for Heaven to live with Thee there.

1. Luke 2:7
Also Luke 2:12

—John McFarland, 1851-1913

HARK! THE HERALD ANGELS SING

—FELIX MENDELSSOHN, 1840

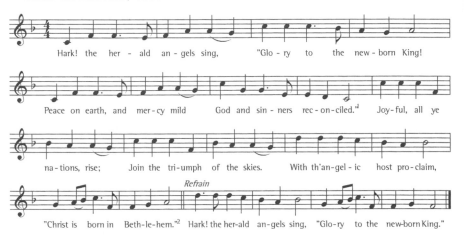

Hark! the her-ald an-gels sing, "Glo-ry to the new-born King!
Peace on earth, and mer-cy mild God and sin-ners rec-on-ciled."[2] Joy-ful, all ye
na-tions, rise; Join the tri-umph of the skies. With th'an-gel-ic host pro-claim,

Refrain

"Christ is born in Beth-le-hem."[2] Hark! the her-ald an-gels sing, "Glo-ry to the new-born King."

2. Christ, by highest Heav'n adored;
   Christ the everlasting Lord;
   Late in time, behold Him come,
   Offspring of a virgin's womb.
   Veiled in flesh the Godhead see;
   Hail th' incarnate Deity,
   Pleased with us in flesh to dwell,[3]
   Jesus our Emmanuel.[4]
   Refrain

3. Hail the heav'nly Prince of Peace![5]
   Hail the Sun of Righteousness!
   Light and life to all He brings,
   Ris'n with healing in His wings.[6]
   Mild He lays His glory by,
   Born that man no more may die.
   Born to raise the sons of earth,
   Born to give them second birth.
   Refrain

4. Come, Desire of nations, come,
   Fix in us Thy humble home;
   Rise, the woman's conqu'ring Seed,[7]
   Bruise in us the serpent's head.
   Now display Thy saving power,
   Ruined nature now restore;
   Now in mystic union join
   Thine to ours, and ours to Thine.
   Refrain

1. Luke 2:14
2. Luke 2:11
3. Philippians 2:6-7
4. Matthew 1:23
5. Isaiah 9:6
6. Malachi 4:2
7. Genesis 3:15

—CHARLES WESLEY, 1739

WE THANK YOU

We thank you for this place in which we dwell,
for the love that unites us,
for the peace accorded us this day,
for the hope with which we expect the morrow,
for the work, the health, the food
and bright skies which make our lives
delightful for our friends in all parts of the earth.

—ROBERT LOUIS STEVENSON, 1850–1894

A PRAYER OF THANKS

Heavenly Father, thank you for sending your Son to earth as a baby
so many years ago. Thank you that He paid the punishment for my
sins by dying on the cross. And thank you that He rose again to
prove that death was truly defeated. I place my trust in You to be
my Savior. Guide me through the dark times of my life and give me
the courage to live for You. Amen.

—MAX LUCADO, *HE STILL MOVES STONES*, 1993

CHRISTMAS CREED

I believe in Jesus Christ and in the beauty of the gospel begun in Bethlehem.

I believe in the one whose spirit glorified a little town; and whose spirit still brings music to persons all over the world, in towns both large and small.

I believe in the one for whom the crowded inn could find no room, and I confess that my heart still sometimes wants to exclude Christ from my life today.

I believe in the one whom the rulers of the earth ignored and the proud could never understand; whose life was among common people, whose welcome came from persons of hungry hearts.

I believe in the one who proclaimed the love of God to be invincible.

I believe in the one whose cradle was a mother's arms, whose modest home in Nazareth had love for its only wealth, who looked at persons and made them see what God's love saw in them, who by love brought sinners back to purity, and lifted human weakness up to meet the strength of God.

I confess my ever-lasting need of God: The need of forgiveness for our selfishness and greed, the need of new life for empty souls, the need of love for hearts grown cold.

I believe in God who gives us the best of himself. I believe in Jesus, the son of the living God, born in Bethlehem this night, for me and for the world.

—ANONYMOUS

O LITTLE TOWN OF BETHLEHEM

—Lewis H. Redner, 1868

O lit-tle town of Beth-le-hem, How stil we see thee lie! A - bove thy deep and

dream-less sleep The si - lent stars go by. Yet in thy dark streets shin - eth The

ev-er-last-ing Light; The hopes and fears of all the years are met in thee to - night.

2. For Christ is born of Mary;
and gathered all above,
while mortals sleep, the angels keep
their watch of wondering love.
O morning stars,[1] together
proclaim the holy birth!
and praises sing to God the King,
and peace to men on earth.[2]

3. How silently, how silently,
the wondrous gift is given!
So God imparts to human hearts
the blessings of his heaven.
No ear may hear his coming,
but in this world of sin,
where meek souls will receive him,
still the dear Christ enters in.[3]

4. O holy Child of Bethlehem,
descend to us, we pray;
cast out our sin and enter in,
be born in us today.
We hear the Christmas angels
the great glad tidings tell;
O come to us, abide with us,
our Lord Emmanuel![4]

1. Job 38:7
2. Luke 2:14
3. Revelation 3:20
4. Isaiah 7:14
Also Micah 5:2

—Phillips Brooks, 1867

A CHRISTMAS BLESSING

God grant you the light in Christmas,
  which is faith;
the warmth of Christmas,
  which is purity;
the righteousness of Christmas,
  which is justice;
the belief in Christmas,
  which is truth;
the all of Christmas,
  which is Christ.

—WILDA ENGLISH, n.d.

SECOND SUNDAY OF CHRISTMAS

*Almighty God, in the birth of your Son you have poured on us the
new light of your incarnate Word, and shown us the fullness of your
love: help us to walk in his light and dwell in his love that we may
know the fullness of his joy; who is alive and reigns with you,
in the unity of the Spirit, one God, now and for ever.*

—THOMAS CRANMER, 1489–1556

JOY TO THE WORLD!

—GEORGE F. HANDEL, 1742

Joy to the world! the Lord is come; Let earth re-ceive her King.[1] Let ev-'ry heart pre-pare Him room, and heav'n and na-ture sing,[2] And heav'n and na-ture sing, And heav'n and heav'n and na-ture sing.

2. Joy to the world! the Savior reigns;
   let us our songs employ,
   while fields and floods, rocks, hills and plains
   repeat the sounding joy,
   repeat the sounding joy,
   repeat, repeat the sounding joy.

3. No more let sins and sorrows grow,
   nor thorns infest the ground;
   He comes to make His blessings flow[3]
   far as the curse is found,
   far as the curse is found,
   far as, far as the curse is found.[4]

4. He rules the world with truth and grace,[5]
   and makes the nations prove
   the glories of His righteousness,
   and wonders of His love,
   and wonders of His love,
   and wonders, wonders of His love.

1. Matthew 12:18
2. Psalm 98:4
3. Galatians 3:13; Luke 4:18-19
4. Genesis 3:17-18
5. Romans 5:12

—ISAAC WATTS, 1719

WHILE SHEPHERDS WATCHED THEIR FLOCKS

—George F. Handel, 1742

While shep-herds watched their flocks by night, All seat-ed on the ground, The an-gel of the Lord came down, And glo-ry shone a - round, And glo-ry shone a - round.[1]

2. "Fear not," said he, for mighty dread
had seized their troubled mind;
"Glad tidings of great joy I bring
to you and all mankind,
to you and all mankind."[2]

3. "To you, in David's town, this day
is born of David's line
a Savior, who is Christ the Lord;
and this shall be the sign,
and this shall be the sign."[3]

4. "The heavenly Babe you there shall find
to human view displayed,
all meanly wrapped in swathing bands,
and in a manger laid,
and in a manger laid."

5. "All glory be to God on high
and to the earth be peace;
good will henceforth from heaven to men
begin and never cease,
begin and never cease."[4]

—Nahum Tate, 1700

1. Luke 2:8-9
2. Luke 2:10
3. Luke 2:11
4. Luke 2:13-14

LORD OF THE CHRISTMASTIDE

The Lord of Christmastide entered into our life by lowly doors. And still He seeks the lowly doors: the door of the workshop, the door of the chamber, and all the unobtrusive doors of human friendship and regard.

—JOHN HENRY JOWETT, 1863–1923

THE LIGHT OF THE WORLD

Jesus, the Light of the World, as we celebrate your birth...may we begin to see the world in the light of understanding you give us. As you chose the lowly, the outcasts, and the poor to receive the greatest news the world had ever known, so may we worship you in meekness of heart. May we also remember our brothers and sisters less fortunate than ourselves in this season of giving. Amen.

—KAREN L. OBERST, 1951–

THE NATIVITY

Among the oxen (like an ox I'm slow)
I see a glory in the stable grow
Which, with the ox's dullness might at length
Give me an ox's strength.

Among the asses (stubborn I as they)
I see my Saviour where I looked for hay;
So may my breast like folly learn at least
The patience of a beast.

Among the sheep (I like a sheep have strayed)
I watch the manger where my Lord is laid;
Oh that my baa-ing nature would win thence
Some woolly innocence!

—C. S. Lewis, 1898–1963

THE FIRST NOEL

—ENGLISH, 1833

The first No - el the an-gels did say Was to cer-tain poor shep-herds in fields as they lay.[1] In fields where they lay keep-ing their sheep on a cold win-ter's night that was so deep. No - el, No - el, No - el, No - el, Born is the King of Is - ra - el!

2. They lookèd up and saw a star
Shining in the east, beyond them far;
And to the earth it gave great light,
And so it continued both day and night.
Refrain

3. And by the light of that same star
Three Wise Men came from country far;
To seek for a King was their intent,
And to follow the star wherever
it went.[2]
Refrain

4. Then entered in those Wise Men three,
Full reverently upon the knee,
And offered there, in His presence,
Their gold and myrrh and
frankincense.[3]
Refrain

5. Then let us all with one accord
Sing praises to our heavenly Lord;
That hath made heaven and earth
of naught,
And with His blood mankind
hath bought.[4]
Refrain

1. Luke 2:8
2. Matthew 2:2
3. Matthew 2:11
4. Revelation 5:9

—OLD ENGLISH CAROL

EPIPHANY

And suddenly—You appeared among us! You could have stood afar off, but You came in vulnerable love, revealing the nature of the Father. You proved once and for all that God's love "reaches to the heavens" by reaching from heaven to us. What an extraordinary act of abounding grace!

Your birth seemed insignificant, even trivial, to most of the world. Yet Simeon prophesied You would be "a light to the Gentiles"... and the Magi were the first to fulfill that word. Overwhelmed by Your royal yet modest love, they tenderly laid gifts at Your feet. They knelt down and worshiped You, "revealing" You to the world as Lord and King.

I will observe these days by asking for a personal epiphany, a sudden revelation of who You really are. By bowing down, laying my gifts at Your feet, and worshiping You, let me "reveal" You as the Savior of all people.

PRAYER OF GLADNESS

Gladly I close this festive day,
Grasping the altar's hallow'd horn;
My slips and faults are washed away,
The Lamb has all my trespass borne.

—CHARLES H. SPURGEON, 1834–1892

BECAUSE ONE CHILD IS BORN

More light than we can learn,
More wealth than we can treasure,
More love than we can earn,
More peace than we can measure,
Because one Child is born.

—CHRISTOPHER FRY, 1907-2005

THE MAGI

Convulsions in the heavens
Have borne one shining word:
A single, silver, sailing star
Declares a royal birth—
And peace to the Jews!
Its tail describes a scepter;
Its rays are coronal.
What can we do but bow before
The child the heavens call—
The King of the Jews.

—WALTER WANGERIN JR. 1944-

FIRST SUNDAY OF EPIPHANY

Eternal Father, who at the baptism of Jesus revealed him to be your Son, anointing him with the Holy Spirit: grant to us, who are born again by water and the Spirit, that we may be faithful to our calling as your adopted children; through Jesus Christ your Son our Lord, who is alive and reigns with you, in the unity of the Holy Spirit, one God, now and for ever. Amen.

—THOMAS CRANMER, 1489–1556

COME AND SEE

In the perfect center of all my circles and of all the spheres of all the world—is Jesus. Here! Come and see! Can you see the tiny baby born? Can you see the Infant King? Can you recognize in him Immanuel? Now you are seeing Christmas.

—WALTER WANGERIN JR. 1944-

WHAT CHILD IS THIS?

—ENGLISH, C. 1642

What Child is this who laid to rest on Mar-y's lap is sleep - ing? Whom

an - gels greet with an - thems sweet[1] While shep - herds watch are keep - ing?[2]

Refrain

This, this is Christ the King, Whom shep - herds guard and an - gels sing.

Haste, haste to bring Him laud,[3] The Babe, the Son of Mar - y.

2. Why lies He in such mean estate,
Where ox and ass are feeding?
Good Christians, fear, for sinners here
The silent Word is pleading.

Nails, spear shall pierce Him through,
The cross be borne for me, for you.
Hail, hail the Word made flesh,[4]
The Babe, the Son of Mary.

3. So bring Him incense, gold and myrrh,[5]
Come peasant, king to own Him;
The King of kings salvation brings,
Let loving hearts enthrone Him.

Raise, raise a song on high,
The virgin sings her lullaby.
Joy, joy for Christ is born,
The Babe, the Son of Mary.

1. Luke 2:13-14
2. Luke 2:15
3. Hebrews 1:6
4. John 1:14
5. Matthew 2:11

—WILLIAM C. DIX, C. 1865

47

O HOLY NIGHT

—Adolph C. Adam, 1847

O Holy night! the stars are brightly shining. It is the night of the dear Savior's birth.

Long lay the world in sin and error pining, Till He appeared and the soul felt its

worth. A thrill of hope the weary world rejoices, For yonder breaks a new and glorious morn!

Fall on your knees! Oh, hear the angel voices![1] O night divine, O

night when Christ was born! O night divine! O night, O night divine!

2. Truly He taught us to love one another;[2]
   His law is love and His Gospel is peace.[3]
   Chains shall He break for the slave is our brother
   And in His Name all oppression shall cease.
   Sweet hymns of joy in grateful chorus raise we,
   Let all within us praise His holy Name!

   Christ is the Lord!
   Oh, praise His name forever!
   His pow'r and glory evermore proclaim![4]
   His pow'r and glory evermore proclaim!

1. Luke 2:13–15
2. John 13:34
3. John 14:27
4. Hebrews 1:6

—Placide Cappeau, 1847; trans. John S. Dwight, 1855

THY PRESENCE

Thy presence fills my mind with peace,
   Brightens the thoughts so dark erewhile,
Bids cares and sad forebodings cease,
   Makes all things smile.

—Charlotte Elliott, 1789–1871

THE STAR OF TRUTH

Thou, O Lord, art the Star of Truth, that riseth out of Jacob, and the man that springeth from Israel. In the new Star Thou showest Thyself as God, and lying in the crib God and Man, we confess thee to be the one Christ. In Thy great mercy grant us the grace of seeing Thee, and show unto us the radiant sign of Thy light, whereby all the darkness of our sins may be put to flight: that so we who now languish with the desire of seeing Thee, may be refreshed with the enjoyment of that blissful vision. Amen.

—Mozarabic Breviary, c. 1775

AS WITH GLADNESS MEN OF OLD

—Konrad Kocher, 1833

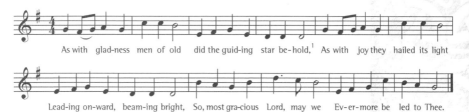

As with glad-ness men of old did the guid-ing star be-hold,[1] As with joy they hailed its light

Lead-ing on-ward, beam-ing bright, So, most gra-cious Lord, may we Ev-er-more be led to Thee.

2. As with joyful steps they sped
   To that lowly manger bed
   There to bend the knee before[2]
   Him Whom Heaven and earth adore;
   So may we with willing feet
   Ever seek Thy mercy seat.

3. As they offered gifts most rare
   At that manger rude and bare;[3]
   So may we with holy joy,
   Pure and free from sin's alloy,
   All our costliest treasures bring,
   Christ, to Thee, our heavenly King.

4. Holy Jesus, every day
   Keep us in the narrow way;
   And, when earthly things are past,
   Bring our ransomed souls at last
   Where they need no star to guide,
   Where no clouds Thy glory hide.[4]

1. Matthew 2:2
2. Matthew 2:11a
3. Matthew 2:11b
4. Revelation 21:23

—William C. Dix, 1860

AN EPIPHANY PRAYER

Father, we thank You for revealing Yourself to us in Jesus the Christ, we who once were not Your people but whom You chose to adopt as Your people. As ancient Israel confessed long ago, we realize that it was not because of our own righteousness, or our own superior wisdom, or strength, or power, or numbers. It was simply because You loved us, and chose to show us that love in Jesus.

As You have accepted us when we did not deserve Your love, will You help us to accept those whom we find it hard to love? Forgive us, O Lord, for any attitude that we harbor that on any level sees ourselves as better or more righteous than others. Will You help us to remove the barriers of prejudice and to tear down the walls of bigotry, religious or social? O Lord, help us realize that the walls that we erect for others only form our own prison.

Will You fill us so full of Your love that there is no more room for intolerance? As You have forgiven us much, will You enable us with Your strength to forgive others even more? Will You enable us through Your abiding Presence among us, communally and individually, to live our lives in a manner worthy of the Name we bear?

May we, through Your guidance and our faithful obedience, find new avenues in ways that we have not imagined of holding the Light of Your love so that it may be a Light of revelation for all people.

We thank You for Your love, praise You for Your Gift, ask for Your continued Presence with us, and bring these petitions in the name of Your Son, who has truly revealed Your heart. Amen.

—DENNIS BRATCHER

BEHOLD YOUR GOD

In seasons of desolation or in seasons of temptation, I would urge you to always learn to withdraw into the inmost chamber of your spirit. There, do nothing but behold God. It is in the depth of your spirit that is the place of true happiness. It is there that the Lord will show you wondrous things.

—Miguel Molinos, 1640–1697

WHAT DIFFERENCE HAS THIS MADE?

The second person of the Trinity lies in the manger for a reason. Because He loves the world, He has come not just to eliminate the peripheral results of man's fall; He is here to cut to the very nerve of man's real dilemma, to solve the problem from which all other problems flow. The "condition of man" is not what modern man thinks it is. Man is a sinner who needs an overwhelming love. Jesus has come to save His people from their sins.

—Francis Schaeffer, 1912–1984

SECOND SUNDAY OF EPIPHANY

Almighty God, in Christ you make all things new: transform the poverty of our nature by the riches of your grace, and in the renewal of our lives make known your heavenly glory; through Jesus Christ your Son our Lord, who is alive and reigns with you, in the unity of the Spirit, one God, now and for ever. Amen.

—Thomas Cranmer, 1489–1556

LOVE DIVINE, ALL LOVES EXCELLING

—JOHN ZUNDEL, 1870

Love di-vine, all loves ex-cel-ling, Joy of heav'n, to earth come down!

Fix in us Thy hum-ble dwell-ing; All Thy faith-ful mer-cies crown.[1]

Je-sus, Thou art all com-pas-sion; Pure, un-bound-ed love Thou art.

Vis-it us with Thy sal-va-tion; En-ter ev-'ry trem-bling heart.

2. Come, Almighty, to deliver,
Let us all Thy life receive;[2]
Suddenly return, and never,
Nevermore Thy temples leave.[3]
Thee we would be always
blessing,[4]
Serve Thee as Thy hosts above,
Pray, and praise Thee without
ceasing,
Glory in Thy perfect love.

3. Finish then Thy new creation;
Pure and spotless let us be;
Let us see Thy great salvation
Perfectly restored in Thee:
Changed from glory into glory,[5]
'Til in heaven we take our
place,
'Til we cast our crowns before
Thee,[6]
Lost in wonder, love, and praise.

1. 2 Corinthians 1:18
2. Romans 8:2
3. Malachi 3:1
4. Psalm 34:1
5. 2 Corinthians 3:18
6. Revelation 4:10

—CHARLES WESLEY, 1747

53

O WORSHIP THE LORD!

O worship the Lord in the beauty of holiness!
Bow down before Him, His glory proclaim;
with gold of obedience, and incense of lowliness,
kneel and adore Him: the Lord is His Name!

—JOHN SAMUEL BEWLEY MONSELL, 1811–1875

SALT AND LIGHT

Lord, as Your Son, the Lord Jesus Christ, was salt and light here on earth, so help us to walk in His way to so serve and minister to the needs of others that we may be salt with flavor and a light set upon a hill. We ask this through Jesus Christ our Lord. Amen.

—ROBERT E. WEBBER, n.d.

FEAR NOT TO ENTER

Fear not to enter His courts in the slenderness
of the poor wealth thou wouldst reckon as thine;
for truth in its beauty, and love in its tenderness,
these are the offerings to lay on His shrine.

These, though we bring them in trembling and fearfulness,
He will accept for the Name that is dear;
mornings of joy give for evenings of tearfulness,
trust for our trembling and hope for our fear.

—JOHN SAMUEL BEWLEY MONSELL, 1811–1875

EPIPHANY

I came searching for You by lead of an extraordinary light,
Thinking, "Surely, my eyes will behold a royal in splendor."
There You were—small, unassuming, vulnerable.

You embarrassed me with your astonishing humility,
Knowing, "Were I such a king, I would expect honor and adoration."
I gave it to You freely—not because You demanded it.... You deserved it.

—JOHN RANDALL DENNIS, 1957-

FAIREST LORD JESUS

—Schlesische Volkslieder, 1842

Fair-est Lord Je - sus! Rul-er of all na - ture! O Thou of God and man the Son!

Thee will I cher - ish; Thee will I hon - or, Thou, my soul's glo - ry, joy, and crown!

2. Fair are the meadows, fairer still the woodlands,
   Robed in the blooming garb of spring;
   Jesus is fairer, Jesus is purer,
   Who makes the woeful heart to sing.[1]

3. Fair is the sunshine, fairer still the moonlight,
   And all the twinkling starry host;
   Jesus shines brighter, Jesus shines purer
   Than all the angels heaven can boast.[2]

4. All fairest beauty, heavenly and earthly,
   Wondrously, Jesus, is found in Thee;
   None can be nearer, fairer or dearer,
   Than Thou, my Savior, art to me.[3]

5. Beautiful Savior! Lord of all the nations!
   Son of God and Son of Man!
   Glory and honor, praise, adoration,
   Now and forever more be Thine.[4]

1. James 5:13
2. Revelation 22:16
3. Psalm 45:2
4. Revelation 5:13

—Munster Gesangbuch, 17th century
trans. Joseph August Seiss

O GOD OF JESUS

O God of Jesus, who dost enfold Thy loving heart and keep with Thy gracious care all manner of men, we praise and bless Thee for our greatest gift, our Saviour Christ. For his glorious birth amid humble folk when the heavenly chorus sang of peace on earth, for His words of life and light, and His blessed ministry, for His death on a cross for our redemption, we give Thee thanks beyond the power of human words to speak.

—GEORGIA HARKNESS, 1891–1974

EPIPHANY

Unclench your fists.
Hold out your hands.
Take mine.
Let us hold each other.
Thus is his Glory
Manifest.

—MADELEINE L'ENGLE, 1918–

THIRD SUNDAY OF EPIPHANY

Almighty God, whose Son revealed in signs and miracles the wonder of your saving presence: renew your people with your heavenly grace, and in all our weakness sustain us by Your mighty power; through Jesus Christ your Son our Lord, who is alive and reigns with you, in the unity of the Spirit, one God, now and for ever. Amen.

—THOMAS CRANMER, 1489–1556

REVEALING CHRIST

For me 'twas not the truth you taught,
To you so clear, to me so dim,
But when you came to see me,
You brought a sense of Him.

And from your eyes He beckons me,
And from your heart His love is shed,
Till I lose sight of you,
And see the Christ instead.

—BEATRICE CLELLAND, n.d.

COMMON, JOYOUS PRAISE

In common, joyous praise to Thee and in contemplation of the mystery of Thy love that has sent us such a Saviour, let all earthly differences be leveled, all human walls cast down. Let our worship with one voice ring true within a fellowship of hearts. So shall Thy name be honored and Thy Son's work be done. In His name we pray. Amen.

—GEORGIA HARKNESS, 1891–1974

CHEERED BY THE PRESENCE OF GOD

Cheered by the presence of God, I will do at each moment, without anxiety, according to the strength which He shall give me, the work that His Providence assigns me. I will leave the rest without concern; it is not my affair.

—FRANÇOIS DE SALIGNAC DE LA MOTHE-FÉNELON, 1651–1715

LOVE SO NEAR

O Thou, in all Thy might so far,
In all Thy love so near,
Beyond the range of sun and star,
And yet beside us here.

What heart can comprehend Thy name,
Or, searching, find Thee out,
Who art within, a quickening flame,
A presence round about?

Yet though I know Thee but in part,
I ask not, Lord, for more:
Enough for me to know Thou art,
To love Thee and adore.

—FREDERICK LUCIAN HOSMER, 1840–1929

PIERCE MY INMOST SOUL

Pierce, O most sweet Lord Jesus, my inmost soul with the most
joyous and healthful wound of Thy love, and with true, calm and
most holy apostolic charity, that my soul may ever languish and
melt with entire love and longing for Thee, may yearn for Thee and
for thy courts, may long to be dissolved and to be with Thee.

—SAINT BONAVENTURE, 1221–1274

LORICA OF SAINT PATRICK

I arise today
Through a mighty strength, the invocation of the Trinity,
Through a belief in the Threeness,
Through confession of the Oneness
Of the Creator of creation.

I arise today
Through the strength of Christ's birth and His baptism,
Through the strength of His crucifixion and His burial,
Through the strength of His resurrection and His ascension,
Through the strength of His descent for the judgment of doom.

I arise today
Through the strength of the love of cherubim,
In obedience of angels,
In service of archangels,
In the hope of resurrection to meet with reward,
In the prayers of patriarchs,
In preachings of the apostles,
In faiths of confessors,
In innocence of virgins,
In deeds of righteous men.

I arise today
Through the strength of heaven;
Light of the sun,
Splendor of fire,
Speed of lightning,
Swiftness of the wind,
Depth of the sea,
Stability of the earth,
Firmness of the rock.

I arise today
Through God's strength to pilot me;
God's might to uphold me,
God's wisdom to guide me,
God's eye to look before me,

God's ear to hear me,
God's word to speak for me,
God's hand to guard me,
God's way to lie before me,
God's shield to protect me,
God's hosts to save me
From snares of the devil,
From temptations of vices,
From every one who desires me ill,
Afar and anear,
Alone or in a multitude.

I summon today all these powers between me and evil,
Against every cruel merciless power that opposes my body and soul,
Against incantations of false prophets,
Against black laws of pagandom,
Against false laws of heretics,
Against craft of idolatry,
Against spells of women and smiths and wizards,
Against every knowledge that corrupts man's body and soul.
Christ shield me today
Against poison, against burning,
Against drowning, against wounding,
So that reward may come to me in abundance.

Christ with me, Christ before me, Christ behind me,
Christ in me, Christ beneath me, Christ above me,
Christ on my right, Christ on my left,
Christ when I lie down, Christ when I sit down,
Christ in the heart of every man who thinks of me,
Christ in the mouth of every man who speaks of me,
Christ in the eye that sees me,
Christ in the ear that hears me.

I arise today
Through a mighty strength, the invocation of the Trinity,
Through a belief in the Threeness,
Through a confession of the Oneness
Of the Creator of creation.

—SAINT PATRICK OF IRELAND, 387–493

FOURTH SUNDAY OF EPIPHANY

God our creator, who in the beginning commanded light to shine out of darkness: we pray that the light of the glorious gospel of Christ may dispel the darkness of ignorance and unbelief, shine into the hearts of all Your people, and reveal the knowledge of Your glory in the face of Jesus Christ Your Son our Lord, who is alive and reigns with You, in the unity of the Spirit, one God, now and for ever. Amen.

—THOMAS CRANMER, 1489–1556

THE VISITATION

Through the tender mercies of our God, the dayspring from on high has visited us. Glory be to Thee, O Lord; glory to you, Creator of light, Enlightener of the world. God is the Lord who has shown us the light.

—LANCELOT ANDREWS, 1555–1626

GRANT MY SOUL HUNGER

Grant that my soul may hunger after Thee, the Bread of Angels, the refreshment of holy souls, our daily and super substantial bread, having all sweetness and savor and every delightful taste. May my heart ever hunger after and feed upon Thee, Whom the angels desire to look upon, and may my inmost soul be filled with the sweetness of Thy savor; may it ever thirst for Thee, the fountain of life, the fountain of wisdom and knowledge, the fountain of eternal light, the torrent of pleasure, the fullness of the house of God; may it ever compass Thee, seek Thee, find Thee, run to Thee, come up to Thee, meditate on Thee, speak of Thee, and do all for the praise and glory of Thy name, with humility and discretion, with love and delight, with ease and affection, with perseverance to the end; and be Thou alone ever my hope, my entire confidence, my riches, my delight, my pleasure, my joy, my rest and tranquility, my peace, my sweetness, my food, my refreshment, my refuge, my help, my wisdom, my portion, my possession, my treasure; in Whom may my mind and my heart be ever fixed and firm and rooted immovably. Amen.

—SAINT BONAVENTURE, 1221–1274

REST

"Rest in the Lord; wait patiently for Him." In Hebrew, "be silent to God, and let Him mould thee." Keep still, and He will mould thee to the right shape.

—MARTIN LUTHER, 1483–1546

GIVE US STEADFAST HEARTS

Give us, O Lord, steadfast hearts that cannot be dragged down by false loves; give us courageous hearts that cannot be worn down by trouble; give us righteous hearts that cannot be sidetracked by unholy or unworthy goals. Give to us also, our Lord and God, understanding to know you, diligence to look for you, wisdom to recognize you, and a faithfulness that will bring us to see you face to face.

—THOMAS À KEMPIS, 1379–1471

ADORATION

You must simplify, de-intellectualize. Put yourself in front of Jesus as a poor man: not with any big ideas, but with living faith. Remain motionless in an act of love before the Father. Don't try to reach God with your understanding; that is impossible. Reach him in love; that is possible.

—CARLO CARRETTO, 1910–1988

LAY THY BURDEN

Low at His feet lay thy burden of carefulness,
high on His heart He will bear it for thee,
and comfort thy sorrows, and answer thy prayerfulness,
guiding thy steps as may best for thee be.

—JOHN SAMUEL BEWLEY MONSELL, 1811–1875

FIFTH SUNDAY OF EPIPHANY

O Lord, we implore You to keep Your Church and household continually in Your true religion; that they who lean only upon the hope of Your heavenly grace may forever be defended by Your mighty power; through Jesus Christ our Lord. Amen.

—THOMAS CRANMER, 1489–1556

ALLELUIA, SONG OF GLADNESS

—SAMUEL WEBBE, 1792

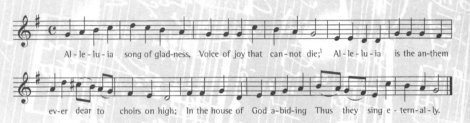

Al - le - lu - ia song of glad-ness, Voice of joy that can - not die;[1] Al - le - lu - ia is the an-them ev-er dear to choirs on high; In the house of God a-bid-ing Thus they sing e - tern-al - ly.

2. Alleluia thou resoundest,
   True Jerusalem and free;
   Alleluia, joyful mother,
   All thy children sing with thee;
   But by Babylon's sad waters
   Mourning exiles now are we.[2]

3. Alleluia we deserve not
   Here to chant forevermore;
   Alleluia our transgressions
   Make us for a while give o'er;
   For the holy time is coming
   Bidding us our sins deplore.

4. Therefore in our hymns we pray Thee,
   Grant us, blessèd Trinity,
   At the last to keep Thine Easter
   In our home beyond the sky;
   There to Thee forever singing
   Alleluia joyfully.

   1. Jeremiah 31:7
   2. Psalm 137:2

   —UNKNOWN, 11TH CENTURY

BURYING THE ALLELUIA

Father, my alleluias fall silent when we consider
Christ's suffering and Your gift of salvation.

Who could look on it and celebrate?
No one can fully stare that agony in the eye and celebrate.

It is as if alleluia has dropped stone cold.
They are dead to me.
But I know there is a resurrection.

Bless us as we enter the season of Lent.

–SOURCE UNKNOWN

LENT

You are the anointed Son of God. You revealed God's nature to us all.

You revealed God, vulnerable and without pretense, in a manger. You showed us God teaching in the temple, amazing rabbis. Because of You, we saw God eagerly asking people, "What can I do for you?" We were surprised to see how delighted He is to respond with a healing touch. You showed us God, welcoming and embracing: "Come to me—I will give you rest." It was God You revealed there, using stories to feed empty souls and filling a multitude of bellies with just a few fish and loaves. We sat on the edge of our seats as we saw You command sea storms and resurrect the dead with a word! You left nothing to description and everything to demonstration.

This begins the sober season when we see You revealing God's nature in completion, leaving nothing to our imaginations. You show us God's love: rugged, whole, no matter how uncomfortable it makes us feel. We are confused when He walks away from all our sensible plans to take a path to certain destruction, His eyes unflinchingly set on Jerusalem.

You show us that God is more than compassionate toward us. You prove God is obsessed with us. You show us He refuses to rest until all things are made new. We watch in horror as You demonstrate that nothing on earth can separate us from His love: not betrayal, denials, mocking, and hateful scourging, not dishonor, not even torturous murder. We delivered up our worst. You show us God, responding with Your best. We are at once joyously amazed and embarrassed.

This changes everything. We can't deceive ourselves any longer with a religion of words, compulsion, ceremony, or acts of piety. We are drawn to worship in genuine adoration and devoted love. I cannot embrace a system of belief or code of behavior. Only a Person who loves us with an outrageous passion can be the object of worship. We worship You!

HERE IS LOVE, VAST AS THE OCEAN

—ROBERT LOWRY, 1876

Here is love, vast as the o - cean, Lov - ing kind - ness as the flood,

When the Prince of Life, our Ran - som, shed for us His pre - cious blood.[1]

Who His love will not re - mem-ber? Who can cease to sing His praise?[2]

He can ne - ver be for - got-ten Through-out heav'n's e - ter-nal days.

2. On the mount of crucifixion,
Fountains opened deep and wide;
Through the floodgates of God's mercy[3]
Flowed a vast and gracious tide.
Grace and love, like mighty rivers,
Poured incessant from above,
And Heav'n's peace and perfect justice[4]
Kissed a guilty world in love.

3. Let me all Thy love accepting,
Love Thee, ever all my days;
Let me seek Thy kingdom only
And my life be to Thy praise;
Thou alone shalt be my glory,[5]
Nothing in the world I see.
Thou hast cleansed and sanctified me,[6]
Thou Thyself hast set me free.[7]

4. In Thy truth Thou dost direct me
By Thy Spirit through Thy Word;
And Thy grace my need is meeting,
As I trust in Thee, my Lord.
Of Thy fullness Thou art pouring
Thy great love and power on me,[8]
Without measure, full and boundless,
Drawing out my heart to Thee.

1. Ephesians 2:13
2. Psalm 61:8
3. Romans 11:29-31
4. Romans 11:33
5. Romans 4:20
6. Ephesians 5:26
7. Galatians 5:1
8. 2 Timothy 1:7

—WILLIAM REES (1802–1883), VV. 1–2
—WILLIAM WILLIAMS (1717–1791), VV. 3–4

NEVER CEASE TO LOVE

Oh my soul, never cease to love and praise this all-gracious Redeemer, whose love is unspeakable, whose riches of grace are unsearchable, whose purchased blessings are eternal. View him in his glory with profoundest adoration.

—THOMAS READE, 1841-1909

INTO THE DARKNESS

Father, we know that in the shadow of Thy great protection no evil can befall us, either in life or after death. Help us then to put our hands in Thine and go into the darkness unafraid.

—GEORGIA HARKNESS, 1891–1974

OUR AMAZING HERO

You amaze us! You could have easily remained in highest heaven, honored by angels, holding on to Your equality with God. Instead, You fearlessly lowered yourself to be conceived by the Spirit. You lowered yourself further to be born in flesh. Further, You chose to submit yourself to suffering; again, lower...to crucifixion. And if that were not low enough, You braved death, burial, and Hades. We believe it all. That's why You are our hero.

—JOHN RANDALL DENNIS, 1957-

THERE IS NONE LIKE YOU

—LENNY LEBLANC, 1991

There is none like you.[1]   No one else can touch my heart like you do.

I could search for all e - ter-ni-ty long   and find   there is none like You. *Fine*

Your mer-cy flows like a riv - ver wide.   And heal-ing comes in Your name.[2]

Suf-fer-ing child - ren are safe   in Your arms   there is none like You. *D.C. al Fine*

1. Psalm 89:8
2. Acts 4:29-30

—LENNY LEBLANC, 1991

THE CHURCH'S ONE FOUNDATION

–SAMUEL SEBASTIAN WESLEY, 1864

The church-'s one foun - da - tion[1] is Je - sus Christ[2] her Lord;[3]

she is his new cre - a - tion by wa - ter and the Word.

From heaven he came and sought her to be his ho - ly bride;

with his own blood he bought her,[4] and for her life he died.

2. Elect from every nation, yet one o'er all the earth,[5]
   Her charter of salvation, one Lord, one faith, one birth;
   One holy Name she blesses, partakes one holy food,
   And to one hope she presses, with every grace endued.

3. Mid toil and tribulation, and tumult of her war
   She waits the consummation of peace for evermore; [6, 7]
   Till with the vision glorious her longing eyes are blessed,
   And the great church victorious shall be the church at rest.

4. Yet she on earth hath union with God, the Three in one,
   And mystic sweet communion with those whose rest is won.
   O happy ones and holy! Lord, give us grace that we
   Like them, the meek and lowly, on high may dwell with Thee.

1. Matthew 16:18
2. 1 Corinthians 3:11
3. Isaiah 28:16
4. Acts 20:28
5. Mark 13:27
6. Matthew 25:1-13
7. Revelation 21:2, 9

–SAMUEL JOHN STONE, 1866

THE APOSTLES' CREED

I believe in God, the Father Almighty,
    the Creator of heaven and earth,
    and in Jesus Christ, His only Son, our Lord:

Who was conceived of the Holy Spirit,
    born of the Virgin Mary,
    suffered under Pontius Pilate,
    was crucified, died, and was buried.

He descended into hell.

The third day He arose again from the dead.

He ascended into heaven
    and sits at the right hand of God the Father Almighty,
    from thence He shall come to judge the living and the dead.

I believe in the Holy Spirit, the holy catholic church,
    the communion of saints,
    the forgiveness of sins,
    the resurrection of the body,
    and the life everlasting.

Amen.

FIRST SUNDAY OF LENT

Almighty God, whose Son Jesus Christ fasted forty days in the wilderness, and was tempted as we are, yet without sin: give us grace to discipline ourselves in obedience to your Spirit; and, as you know our weakness, so may we know your power to save; through Jesus Christ your Son our Lord, who is alive and reigns with you, in the unity of the Spirit, one God, now and for ever. Amen.

—THOMAS CRANMER, 1489–1556

THE GOD WHO CARES

Everlasting and merciful God, who has not spared Thine own Son but hath given Him up for us all, that He should bear our sins upon the cross, grant that our hearts may never be disturbed or discouraged in this faith.

—MARTIN LUTHER, 1483–1546

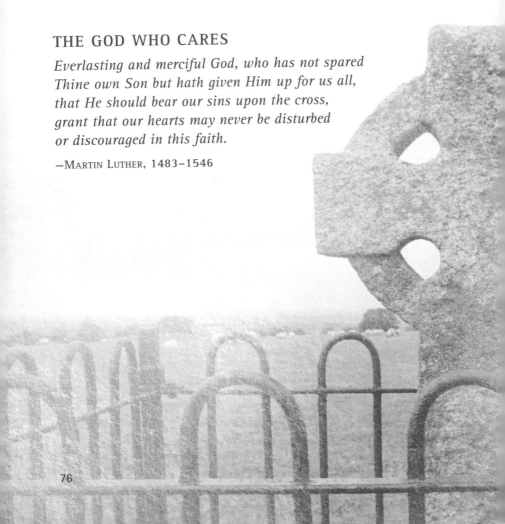

WHEN I SURVEY THE WONDROUS CROSS

—Lowell Mason, 1824

When I sur-vey the won-drous cross on which the

Prince of Glo-ry died,[1] my rich-est gain I count but

loss,[2] and pour con-tempt on all my pride.

2. Forbid it, Lord, that I should boast,[3]
   Save in the death of Christ my God!
   All the vain things that charm me most,
   I sacrifice them to His blood.

1. Acts 3:15
2. Philippians 3:7
3. Galatians 6:14

3. See from His head, His hands, His feet,
   Sorrow and love flow mingled down!
   Did e'er such love and sorrow meet,
   Or thorns compose so rich a crown?

4. His dying crimson, like a robe,
   Spreads o'er His body on the tree;
   Then I am dead to all the globe,
   And all the globe is dead to me.

5. Were the whole realm of nature mine,
   That were a present far too small;
   Love so amazing, so divine,
   Demands my soul, my life, my all.

—Isaac Watts, 1707

LENTEN PRAYER OF SAINT EPHREM

O Lord and Master of my life! Take from me the spirit of sloth, faint-heartedness, lust of power, and idle talk. But give rather the spirit of chastity, humility, patience, and love to Thy servant. Yea, O Lord and King! Grant me to see my own errors and not to judge my brother; for Thou art blessed unto ages of ages. Amen.

—SAINT EPHREM THE SYRIAN, C. 306–373

YOU ARE GOOD AND MERCIFUL

You, Lord, are good and merciful, and Your right hand has respected the depth of my death and, from the bottom of my heart, has emptied that abyss of corruption. And Your whole gift to me was not to will what I willed, and to will what You willed. But where was my free will through all those years, and out of what low and deep recess was my free will called forth in a moment so I could submit my neck to Your easy yoke, and my shoulders to Your light burden, Christ Jesus, my Helper and Redeemer?

—SAINT AUGUSTINE OF HIPPO, 354–430

INFINITE FULLNESS IN CHRIST

O Lord, seeing there is in Christ Jesus an infinite fullness of all that we can want or wish, O that we may all receive of His fullness, grace upon grace; grace to pardon our sins and subdue our iniquities; to justify our persons and to sanctify our souls. O make us partakers of the inheritance of Thy saints. Amen.

—JOHN WESLEY, 1703–1791

MY HOPE IS BUILT ON NOTHING LESS

—William B. Bradbury, 1863

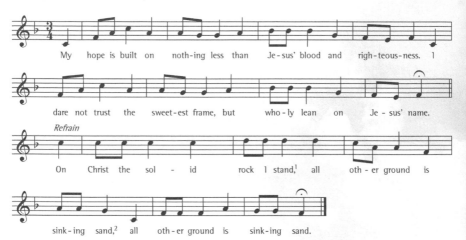

My hope is built on noth-ing less than Je-sus' blood and righ-teous-ness. I

dare not trust the sweet-est frame, but who-ly lean on Je-sus' name.

Refrain

On Christ the sol - id rock I stand,[1] all oth-er ground is

sink-ing sand,[2] all oth-er ground is sink-ing sand.

2. When darkness seems to hide His face,
   I rest on His unchanging grace.
   In every high and stormy gale,
   My anchor holds within the veil. [3]
   Refrain

3. His oath, His covenant, His blood,
   Support me in the whelming flood.
   When all around my soul gives way,
   He then is all my Hope and Stay.
   Refrain

4. When He shall come with trumpet sound, [4]
   Oh may I then in Him be found.[5]
   Dressed in His righteousness alone, [6]
   Faultless to stand before the throne.
   Refrain

1. Psalm 125:1
2. Psalm 40:2
3. Hebrews 6:19
4. 1 Corinthians 15:52
5. 1 Thessalonians 4:17
6. Isaiah 61:10

—EDWARD MOTE, 1834

GIVE THANKS

—HENRY SMITH, 1978

Give thanks with a grate-ful heart;[1] Give thanks to the Ho - ly One;

Give thanks be-cause He's giv-en Je - sus Christ, His Son.

Give thanks with a grate-ful heart; Give thanks to the Ho - ly One;

Give thanks be-cause He's giv-en Je - sus Christ, His Son.

And now let the weak say, "I am strong;"[2] let the poor say, "I am rich," be-cause of

what the Lord has done for us and us. Give thanks!

1. Psalm 145:10
2. Joel 3:10

—HENRY SMITH, 1978

WE THANK THEE, LORD

Almighty God, unto whom all hearts are open, Thou knowest the sinful, sorrowing hearts of men. And Thou who knowest all has come among us in Thy blessed Son to bear our grief, to carry our sorrows, to heal the wounds of our transgressions! We thank Thee, Lord.

—GEORGIA HARKNESS, 1891–1974

CAST YOURSELF UPON HIM

Why do you stand on yourself and in that way not stand at all? Cast yourself upon Him; fear not, He will not withdraw Himself so that you will fall; cast yourself fearlessly upon Him. He will receive and will heal you.

—SAINT AUGUSTINE OF HIPPO, 354–430

SECOND SUNDAY OF LENT

Almighty God, you show those who are in error the light of your truth, that they may return to the way of righteousness: grant to all those who are admitted into the fellowship of Christ, that they may reject things that are contrary to their profession, and follow all such things as are agreeable to the same; through our Lord Jesus Christ, who is alive and reigns with you, in the unity of the Spirit, one God, now and for ever. Amen.

—THOMAS CRANMER, 1489–1556

GIVE ME JESUS

–Spiritual

Dark mid-night was my cry, Dark mid-night was my cry,
Dark mid-night was my cry. Give me Je - sus.

Refrain
Give me Je - sus! Give me Je - sus You can have all this
world give me Je - sus.

2. In the morning when I rise,
   In the morning when I rise,
   In the morning when I rise,
   Give me Jesus.
        Refrain

3. O, when I am alone,
   O, when I am alone,
   O, when I am alone,
   Give me Jesus.
        Refrain

4. And when I come to die,
   And when I come to die,
   And when I come to die,
   Give me Jesus.
        Refrain

–Spiritual

THE JOYOUS EMBRACE

It was for joy You suffered it all. You knew full well the death You would encounter. But for the joy that was set before You, You walked right into it—radiant. And what was the prize our Champion was given for His victory? A bunch of rebellious, captive enemies! But Your love is so great, it didn't matter. It just came rushing over our sins like a tsunami. And Your response to our ingratitude? A joyous embrace!

—JOHN RANDALL DENNIS, 1957-

A HAPPY LIFE

How then do I seek You, Lord? When I seek You, my God, I seek a happy life. I will seek You so that my soul will live. My body lives by my soul, and my soul by You.

—SAINT AUGUSTINE OF HIPPO, 354–430

MORE ABUNDANTLY

Freedom! The only way to consider Your passion without debilitating remorse is to see the freedom You purchased through suffering. Indeed, freedom is the reason You set us free. I can honor Your sacrifice most by reveling in the life of freedom You bought me. To drink in an abundant life deeply, to sing, to embrace abundance wearing joy and dance freely in it, to laugh until my sides hurt. If I neglect the abundant life You purchased, Your sacrifice would be in vain.

—JOHN RANDALL DENNIS, 1957-

I WILL SING OF MY REDEEMER

—JAMES McGRANAHAN, 1877

2. I will tell the wondrous story,
   How my lost estate to save,
   In His boundless love and mercy,
   He the ransom freely gave.[3]
   Refrain

3. I will praise my dear Redeemer,
   His triumphant power I'll tell,[4]
   How the victory He giveth
   Over sin, and death, and hell.[5]
   Refrain

4. I will sing of my Redeemer,
   And His heav'nly love to me;
   He from death to life hath
           brought me,
   Son of God with Him to be.
   Refrain

1. Galatians 3:13
2. Ephesians 1:7
3. Mark 10:45
4. Job 19:21
5. 1 Corinthians 15:54-57

—PHILIP P. BLISS, 1876

DESTROY THE POWER OF THE DEVIL!

O Savior of the world, Thou that hast destroyed the power of the devil, that hast overcome death, that sitteth at the right hand of the Father, Thou that wilt speedily come down in Thy Father's glory to judge all men according to their works; be Thou my light and peace. Destroy the power of the devil in me and make me a new creature. Amen.

—JOHN WESLEY, 1703–1791

SAVE US!

Out of the depths, O Lord, we cry unto Thee. Save us lest we perish in our own indifference and despair. Forgive our iniquities; strengthen us for our labors; confirm us in a faith that cannot be shaken. Through Jesus Christ our Lord. Amen.

—GEORGIA HARKNESS, 1891–1974

LORD, HAVE MERCY

–STEVE MERKEL, 2000

2. I have built an altar where I worship things of man.
   I have taken journeys that have drawn me far from You.
   Now I am returning to Your mercies ever flowing.
   Pardon my transgressions, help me love You again.
       Refrain

1. 1 John 1:9
2. Luke 18:38
3. Luke 1:78
4. Psalm 25:7

3. I have longed to know You and all Your tender mercies,[3]
   Like a river of forgiveness ever flowing without end.
   So I bow my heart before You in the goodness of Your presence,[4]
   Your grace forever shining like a beacon in the night.
       Refrain

–STEVE MERKEL, 2000

BRING US BACK TO YOU

Lord, our God, you formed man from the clay of the earth and breathed into him the spirit of life, but he turned from your face and sinned. In this time of repentance we call out for your mercy. Bring us back to you and to the life your Son won for us by his death on the cross, for he lives and reigns for ever and ever. Amen.

—UNKNOWN

THIRD SUNDAY OF LENT

Almighty God, whose dear Son went not up to joy but first he suffered pain, and entered not into glory before he was crucified: mercifully grant that we, walking in the way of the cross, may find it none other than the way of life and peace; through Jesus Christ your Son our Lord, who is alive and reigns with you, in the unity of the Spirit, one God, now and for ever. Amen.

—THOMAS CRANMER, 1489–1556

TEACH US

O God most holy, whose thoughts are not our thoughts and whose ways are not our ways, teach us to think Thy thoughts after Thee and to walk in Thy ways.

—GEORGIA HARKNESS, 1891–1974

HELP OUR UNBELIEF

Thou hast sent Thine only Son that whosoever believeth in Him should not perish but have everlasting life. O Lord, we believe, help our unbelief. Give us true repentance toward God and faith in our Lord Jesus Christ, and let the love of God be shed in our hearts by the Holy Ghost which is given us.

—JOHN WESLEY, 1703–1791

GRANT US GRACE TO HEAR

Almighty God, grant us grace to hear Jesus Christ, the heavenly bread, preached throughout the world and truly to understand Him. May all evil, heretical and human doctrines be cut off, while Thy word as the living bread be distributed.

—MARTIN LUTHER, 1483–1546

ONLY BY GRACE

–GERRIT GUSTAFSON, 1990

On-ly by grace can we en - ter On-ly by grace can we stand,

not by our hu - man en - deav - or, but by the blood of the Lamb.

In - to Your pres - ence You call us, You call us to come.

3rd time to Coda

In - to Your pres - ence You draw us, and now by Your grace we come.

come and now by Your grace we come. Lord, if you mark our trans-gress -

ions who would stand?[1] Thanks to Your grace we are cleansed

D.C. al Coda

by the blood of the Lamb.

come, and now by Your grace we come and now by Your grace we come.

1. Psalm 130:3

–GERRIT GUSTAFSON, 1990

OPEN OUR EYES

Almighty God, by the power of your Holy Spirit open our eyes, ears, hearts, and very lives to your presence so that today we may worship and serve you in faithfulness, be blessing and healing reminders of your love to all whose lives we touch. We offer our prayers in the name of Christ. Amen.

—RUBEN P. JOB AND NORMAN SHAWCHUCK, n.d.

TEACH ME, O LORD, TO PRAY

Listen, O Lord, to my prayers. Listen to my desire to be with you, to dwell in your house, and let my whole being be filled with your presence. But none of this is possible without you. When you are not the one who fills me, I am soon filled with endless thoughts and concerns that divide me and tear me away from you. Even thoughts about you, good spiritual thoughts, can be little more than distractions when you are not their author.

But Lord, let me at least remain open to your initiative; let me wait patiently and attentively for that hour when you will come and break through all the walls I have erected. Teach me, O Lord, to pray.

—HENRI J. M. NOUWEN, 1932–1996

AS PANTS THE HART

As pants the hart for cooling streams
When heated in the chase,
So longs my soul, O God, for Thee
And Thy refreshing grace.

For Thee, my God, the living God,
My thirsty soul doth pine;
Oh, when shall I behold Thy face,
Thou Majesty Divine?

Why restless, why cast down, my soul?
Hope still; and thou shalt sing
The praise of Him who is thy God,
Thy health's eternal Spring.

To Father, Son, and Holy Ghost,
The God whom we adore,
Be glory as it was, is now,
And shall be evermore.

—NAHUM TATE AND NICHOLAS BRADY, 1696

FOURTH SUNDAY OF LENT

Merciful Lord, absolve your people from their offences, that through your bountiful goodness we may be delivered from the chains of those sins which by our frailty we have committed; grant this, heavenly Father, for Jesus Christ's sake, our blessed Lord and Savior, who is alive and reigns with you, in the unity of the Spirit, one God, now and for ever. Amen.

—THOMAS CRANMER, 1489–1556

WITH A LOVE LIKE THIS,
YOU CAN PRAY VERY SIMPLY...

Our Father in heaven,
Reveal who you are.
Set the world right;
Do what's best—
    as above, so below.
Keep us alive with three square meals.
Keep us forgiven with you and forgiving others.
Keep us safe from ourselves and the Devil.
You're in charge!
You can do anything you want!
You're ablaze in beauty!
Yes. Yes. Yes.

—TRANSLITERATION OF MATTHEW 6:9-13 *THE MESSAGE*,
    BY EUGENE H. PETERSON

OUR FATHER

–John Randall Dennis, 1994

Our Fa-ther who art in hea-ven, hal-lowed it be Thy name. Thy king-dom come, Thy will be done on earth as it is in heav - en. Give us our dai - ly bread. For-give us as we for - give. And lead us not in to wrong. De - liv-er us from all e - vil. For Thine is the king-dom, Thine is the power. Thine is the glo-ry for-ev - er and ev - er.

—Adapted from Matthew 6

A HYMN TO GOD THE FATHER (I)

Wilt Thou forgive that sin where I begun,
   Which was my sin, though it were done before?
Wilt Thou forgive that sin, through which I run,
   And do run still, though still I do deplore?
When Thou hast done, Thou hast not done,
   For I have more.

—JOHN DONNE, 1572–1631

A HYMN TO GOD THE FATHER (II)

Wilt Thou forgive that sin which I have won
   Others to sin, and made my sin their door?
Wilt Thou forgive that sin which I did shun
   A year or two, but wallowed in a score?
When Thou hast done, Thou hast not done,
   For I have more.

—JOHN DONNE, 1572–1631

A HYMN TO GOD THE FATHER (III)

I have a sin of fear, that when I have spun
   My last thread, I shall perish on the shore;
But swear by Thyself, that at my death Thy Son
   Shall shine as he shines now, and heretofore;
And having done that, Thou hast done;
   I fear no more.

—JOHN DONNE, 1572–1631

IN YOUR WILL

Lord Jesus, keep me in Your will. Don't let me go mad by poking about outside it.

—CORRIE TEN BOOM, 1892–1983

A HEART OF FLESH

O Lord, who hast mercy upon all, take away from me my sins, and mercifully kindle in me the fire of thy Holy Spirit. Take away from me the heart of stone, and give me a heart of flesh, a heart to love and adore Thee, a heart to delight in Thee, to follow and enjoy Thee, for Christ's sake. Amen.

—SAINT AMBROSE OF MILAN, 339–397

FIFTH SUNDAY OF LENT

Merciful God, who by the death and resurrection of your Son Jesus Christ delivered and saved the world: grant that by faith in him who suffered on the cross we may triumph in the power of his victory; through Jesus Christ your Son our Lord, who is alive and reigns with you, in the unity of the Spirit, one God, now and for ever. Amen.

—THOMAS CRANMER, 1489–1556

ENLARGE MY HOUSE

O Lord, the house of my soul is narrow; enlarge it that You may enter in. It is ruinous, O repair it! It displeases Your sight. I confess it, I know. But who shall cleanse it, to whom shall I cry but to You? Cleanse me from my secret faults, O Lord, and spare Your servant from strange sins.

—SAINT AUGUSTINE OF HIPPO, 354–430

YOURS IS SALVATION

For yours is salvation, and from you is redemption, and by your right hand is restoration, and your finger is fortification. Your command is justification. Your mercy is liberation. Your countenance is illumination. Your face is exultation. Your spirit is benefaction. Your anointing oil is consolation. A dew drop of your grace is exhilaration. You give comfort. You make us forget despair. You lift away the gloom of grief. You change the sighs of our heart into laughter. To you is fitting blessing with praise in heaven and on earth from our forefathers and unto all their generations forever and ever. Amen.

—SAINT GREGORY OF NAREK, 950–1003

THY LOVINGKINDNESS

—Hugh Mitchell, 1962

Thy lov-ing-kind-ness is bet-ter than life, Thy lov-ing-kind-ness is bet-ter than life My lips shall praise Thee, thus will I bless Thee: I will lift up my hands un-to Thy name.

2. I will lift up my hands to Thy name,
   I will lift up my hands to Thy name.
   My lips shall praise Thee, thus will I bless Thee—
   I will lift up my hands unto Thy name.

—Adapted from Psalm 63
—Hugh Mitchell, 1962

I HAVE TO DIE

*Yes, Lord, I have to die—with you, through you, and in you—
and thus become ready to recognize you when you appear to
me in your Resurrection. There is so much in me that needs
to die: false attachments, greed and anger, impatience and
stinginess.... I see clearly now how little I have died with
you, really gone your way and been faithful to it. O Lord,
make this Lenten season different from the other ones. Let
me find you again. Amen.*

—HENRI J. M. NOUWEN, 1932–1996

IN SUFFERING

*Father, let this suffering pass from me; yet not my will but
yours be done. May you be blessed forever. Jesus, Son of
God, have mercy on me. With you I am nailed to the cross.
Let my pains be mingled with yours for the saving of the
world. Holy Spirit, comforter and consoler, heal what is ill in
me, strengthen what is weak, sweeten what is sour or
cranky. Save me from depression and self-pity; renew my
courage; bring me to pray with Jesus on the cross: Father,
into your hands I commend my spirit. Amen.*

—THE REDEMPTORIST MISSION PRAYER BOOK, 1988

PRAYER OF ABANDONMENT

*Father, I abandon myself into your hands;
do with me whatever you will. Whatever you
may do, I thank you. I am ready for all, I
accept all. Let only your will be done in me,
and in all your creatures. I wish no more
than this, O Lord. Into your hands I commend my spirit; I offer it to you, Lord, and
so need to give myself, to surrender myself
into your hands, without reserve and with
boundless confidence, for you are my Father.*

—CHARLES DE FOUCALD, 1858–1916

I SURRENDER ALL

—Winfield S. Weeden, 1896

All to Je - sus I sur-ren - der; all to him I free - ly give;

I will ev - er love and trust him, in his pres - ence dai - ly live.

Refrain

I sur-ren - der all, I sur-ren - der all,

all to thee, my bless - ed Sav - ior, I sur-ren - der all.[1]

2. All to Jesus I surrender;
   Humbly at his feet I bow,
   Worldly pleasures all forsaken;
   Take me, Jesus, take me now.[2]
      Refrain

3. All to Jesus, I surrender;
   Make me, Savior, wholly thine;[3]
   Let me feel the Holy Spirit,
   Truly know that thou art mine.
      Refrain

4. All to Jesus, I surrender;
   Lord, I give myself to thee;
   Fill me with thy love and power;[4]
   Let thy blessing fall on me.
      Refrain

5. All to Jesus I surrender;
   Now I feel the sacred flame.
   O the joy of full salvation!
   Glory, glory, to his name!
      Refrain

1. John 12:25
2. Romans 6:13
3. Romans 12:1
4. 2 Timothy 1:7

—Judson W. Van DeVenter, 1896

Lent

BEFORE THE THRONE OF GOD ABOVE

—Vicki Cook, 1993

Be fore the throne of God a - bove, I have a strong and per-fect plea, a great High Priest whose name is Love,[1] Who ev - er lives and pleads for me.[2] My name is gra-ven on his hands, my name is writ-ten on his heart. I know that while in heav'n He stands no tongue can bid me thence de - part, no tongue can bid me thence de - part.

2. When Satan tempts me to despair
And tells me of the guilt within,
Upward I look and see Him there
Who made an end of all my sin.

Because the sinless Savior died
My sinful soul is counted free.[3]
For God the just is satisfied
To look on Him and pardon me,
To look on Him and pardon me.

3. Behold Him there the risen Lamb,
   My perfect spotless righteousness,[4]
   The great unchangeable I AM,
   King of glory and of grace.[5]

   One in Himself I cannot die.
   My soul is purchased by His blood,
   My life is hid with Christ on high,[6]
   With Christ my Savior and my God!
   With Christ my Savior and my God!

1. Hebrews 4:14
2. Romans 8:33-34
3. Ephesians 1:7
4. 1 Peter 1:18-20
5. Psalm 24:10
6. Colossians 3:3

—Charitie L. Bancroft, 1863

GOD SUFFERS

I cannot think that God could be content
To view unmoved the toiling and the strain,
The groaning of the ages, sick and spent,
The whole creation travailing in pain.
The suffering God is no vast cosmic force,
That by some blind, unthinking, loveless power
Keeps stars and atoms swinging in their course,
And reckons naught of men in this grim hour.
Nor is the suffering God a fair ideal
That comes to birth within a valiant heart,
A figment of the mind to help me steel
My soul to pain and play a manly part.
God suffers with a love that cleanses dross;
A God like that, I see upon a cross.

—GEORGIA HARKNESS, 1891–1974

GOD SO LOVED THE WORLD

—JOHN STAINER, 1887

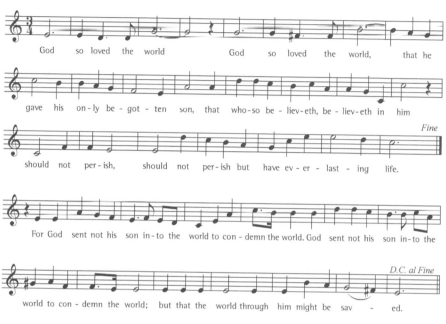

—ADAPTED FROM JOHN 3:16-17

PALM SUNDAY

Almighty and everlasting God, who in your tender love towards the human race sent your Son our Savior Jesus Christ to take upon him our flesh and to suffer death upon the cross: grant that we may follow the example of his patience and humility, and also be made partakers of his resurrection; through Jesus Christ your Son our Lord, who is alive and reigns with you, in the unity of the Spirit, one God, now and for ever. Amen.

—Thomas Cranmer, 1489–1556

HOLY WEEK

*No other single week brings us so many different emotions,
Lord. We are humbled, embarrassed, broken, and overjoyed
all at once. And our words cannot convey what is in our hearts.
Let the Spirit communicate for us our love, our gratitude, our
heartfelt devotion.*

CLEANSE THIS TEMPLE

Enter my doors. Overturn my tables. Throw out robbers that have no place in my courts. Make your Father's temple a house of prayer.

—John Randall Dennis, 1957-

VIOLENT GRACE

So ruthless, He loves us,
So reckless His embrace
to show relentless kindness, to a hardened human race.
The joy that was before Him
On the Man of Sorrows' face,
And by His blood He bought a violent grace.

—Michael Card, 1957-

BREAD OF THE WORLD

—JOHN S. B. HODGES, 1868

Bread of the World in mer - cy bro - ken,[1] wine of the soul in

mer - cy shed,[2] by whom the words of life were spo - ken,

and in whose death our sins are dead.

2. Look on the heart by sorrow broken,[3]
   Look on the tears by sinners shed;
   And be Thy feast to us the token,
   That by Thy grace our souls are fed.

1. John 6:51
2. Matthew 26:27-28
3. Isaiah 53:2-4

—REGINALD HEBER, 1827

THE LAST SUPPER

Lord Jesus,
once in the wilderness
your people ate heavenly manna
and they were filled.
And once in a desert place
you fed the hungry
with blessed bread.
A simple thing, we say,
costing our mighty God
little effort.

But what if bread is
a body offered for all,
and a cup of wine
your own life-blood
given to those who hardly care?

A costly thing, we say,
Is there anything more
God could have done?
Anything more
Love could do
than lay down his life
for his friends?

—UNKNOWN

A PRAYER FOR
MAUNDY THURSDAY

*Christ, whose feet were caressed
with perfume and a woman's hair,
you humbly took basin and towel
and washed the feet of your friends.
Wash us also in your tenderness as
we touch one another; that,
embracing your service freely, we
may accept no other bondage in
your name. Amen.*

—UNKNOWN

AND CAN IT BE?

–THOMAS CAMPBELL, 1825

And can it be that I should gain An in - t'rest in the Sa - vior's blood? Died He for me, who caused His pain? For me, who Him to death pur - sued? A - maz - ing love! How can it be that Thou, my God, shouldst die for me?

2. He left His Father's throne above
   So free, so infinite His grace—
   Emptied Himself of all but love,
   And bled for Adam's helpless race:[1]
   'Tis mercy all, immense and free,
   For O my God, it found out me!
   'Tis mercy all, immense and free,
   For O my God, it found out me!

3. Long my imprisoned spirit lay,
   Fast bound in sin and nature's night;
   Thine eye diffused a quickening ray—
   I woke, the dungeon flamed with light;
   My chains fell off, my heart was free,
   I rose, went forth, and followed Thee.
   My chains fell off, my heart was free,
   I rose, went forth, and followed Thee.

4. No condemnation now I dread;[2]
   Jesus, and all in Him, is mine;
   Alive in Him, my living Head,[3]
   And clothed in righteousness divine,[4]
   Bold I approach th'eternal throne,
   And claim the crown,[5] through Christ my own.[6]
   Bold I approach th'eternal throne,
   And claim the crown, through Christ my own.

1. Romans 5:6-8
2. Romans 8:1
3. Ephesians 4:15
4. Revelation 19:8
5. 2 Timothy 4:8
6. 1 Thessalonians 5:9

—CHARLES WESLEY, 1738

115

YOU DID THIS FOR ME?

The diadem of pain
which sliced your gentle face,
three spikes piercing flesh and wood
to hold you in your place.

The need for blood I understand.
Your sacrifice I embrace.
But the bitter sponge, the cutting spear,
the spit upon your face?
Did it have to be a cross?
Did not a kinder death exist
than six hours hanging between
   life and death,
all spurred by a betrayer's kiss?

"Oh, Father," you pose,
heart-stilled at what could be,
"I'm sorry to ask, but I long to know,
did you do this for me?"

—MAX LUCADO, 1955-

THE FATHER'S HANDS
*Father, into your hands I commit my spirit. For it is your business,
not mine. You will know every shade of my suffering; You will care
for me with your perfect fatherhood.*

—GEORGE MACDONALD, 1824–1905

O SACRED HEAD, NOW WOUNDED

–HANS L. HASSLER, 1601

O sa - cred Head, now wound - ded, with grief and shame weighed down,

now scorn - ful - ly sur - round - ed with thorns, Thine on - ly crown![1]

how pale Thou art with an - guish, with sore a - buse and scorn!

How does that vis - age lan - guish which once was bright as morn![2]

2. What Thou, my Lord, hast suffered, was all for sinners' gain;
   Mine, mine was the transgression, but Thine the deadly pain.[3]
   Lo, here I fall, my Savior! 'Tis I deserve Thy place;
   Look on me with Thy favor, vouchsafe to me Thy grace.

3. What language shall I borrow to thank Thee, dearest friend,
   For this Thy dying sorrow, Thy pity without end?
   O make me Thine forever, and should I fainting be,
   Lord, let me never, never outlive my love to Thee.

4. My Shepherd, now receive me; my Guardian, own me Thine.
   Great blessings Thou didst give me, O source of gifts divine.
   Thy lips have often fed me with words of truth and love;
   Thy Spirit oft hath led me to heavenly joys above.

1. Matthew 27:29
2. Isaiah 52:14
3. Isaiah 53:5

5. The joy can never be spoken, above all joys beside,
   When in Thy body broken I thus with safety hide.
   O Lord of Life, desiring Thy glory now to see,
   Beside Thy cross expiring, I'd breathe my soul to Thee.

–BERNARD OF CLAIRVAUX, 1153

ABOVE ALL

—PAUL BALOCHE AND LENNY LEBLANC, 1999

A-bove all   pow-ers,   a-bove all kings[1] a-bove all na - ture and all cre - a - ted
kingdoms,   a-bove all thrones   a- bove all won-ders   the world has ev - er

things. A - bove all   wis - dom   and all the ways   of man,
known A - bove all   wealth   and trea-sures of   the earth.

You were here be-fore the world be-gan[2] A- bove all There's no way to mea - sure what You're worth.

Cru - ci -fied   laid be-hind   a stone.[3]   You   lived to die   re -

ject-ed and   a-lone[4] Like a rose   tramp-led on   the ground,   You took   the fall

and thought   of me   a-bove all.

1. John 3:31
2. John 1:1-5
3. John 19:18
4. 1 Peter 2:3-5

—PAUL BALOCHE AND LENNY LEBLANC, 1999

CHRIST THE LORD IS RISEN TODAY

—UNKNOWN

Christ the Lord is risen to day, Al – – – le – lu – ia!

Earth and heaven in cho - rus say, Al – – – le – lu – ia!

Raise your joys and tri - umphs high, Al – – le – lu – ia!

Sing, ye heav-ens, and earth re - ply, Al – – – le – lu – ia!

2. Love's redeeming work is done, Alleluia!
   Fought the fight, the battle won, Alleluia!
   Lo! the Sun's eclipse is over, Alleluia!
   Lo! He sets in blood no more, Alleluia!

3. Lives again our glorious King, Alleluia!
   Where, O death, is now thy sting? Alleluia![1]
   Once He died our souls to save, Alleluia!
   Where thy victory, O grave? Alleluia![2]

4. Soar we now where Christ hath led, Alleluia!
   Following our exalted Head, Alleluia!
   Made like Him, like Him we rise, Alleluia!
   Ours the cross, the grave, the skies, Alleluia!

1. 1 Corinthians 15:55
2. 1 Corinthians 15:56-57

—CHARLES WESLEY, 1739

HOLY SATURDAY

O God, Creator of heaven and earth: Grant that just as the crucified body of your dear Son was laid in the tomb and rested on this holy Sabbath, so may we await with him the coming of the third day and rise with him to newness of life; he who now lives and reigns with you and the Holy Spirit, one God, for ever and ever. Amen.

—THOMAS CRANMER, 1489-1556

JESUS! WHAT A FRIEND FOR SINNERS

—Rowland H. Prichard, 1830

Je - sus! What a friend for sin - ners![1] Je - sus lov - er of my soul!

Friends may fail me, foes as - sail me. He, my Sav - ior, makes me whole.

Refrain

Hal - le - lu - jah! What a Sav - ior! Hal - le - lu - jah! What a Friend!

Sav - ing, help - ing, keep - ing, lov - ing, He is with me to the end.

2. Jesus! What a Strength in weakness!
   Let me hide myself in Him.
   Tempted, tried, and sometimes failing,
   He, my Strength, my victory wins.[2]
   Refrain

3. Jesus! What a Help in sorrow!
   While the billows over me roll,
   Even when my heart is breaking,
   He, my Comfort, helps my soul.
   Refrain

1. Luke 7:34
2. Titus 2:13-14
3. Colossians 1:13-15

4. Jesus! What a Guide and Keeper!
   While the tempest still is high,
   Storms about me, night overtakes me,
   He, my Pilot, hears my cry.
   Refrain

5. Jesus! I do now receive Him,
   More than all in Him I find.
   He hath granted me forgiveness,[3]
   I am His, and He is mine.
   Refrain

—J. Wilbur Chapman, 1910

121

JESUS PAID IT ALL

—JOHN THOMAS GRAPE, 1865

I hear the Sav-ior say, "Thy strength in-deed is small;

Child of weak - ness watch and pray,[1] Find in Me thine all in all." [2]

Refrain

Je - sus paid it all,[3] all to Him I owe;

Sin had left a crim-son stain, He washed it white as snow.

2. For nothing good have I
   Whereby Thy grace to claim,[4]
   I'll wash my garments white[5]
   In the blood of Calv'ry's Lamb.
   Refrain

3. Lord, now indeed I find
   Thy power and Thine alone,
   Can change the leper's spots
   And melt the heart of stone.
   Refrain

4. And when before the throne
   I stand in Him complete,
   "Jesus died my soul to save"
   My lips shall still repeat.
   Refrain

1. Matthew 26:41
2. Colossians 3:11
3. 1 Corinthians 7:23
4. Romans 11:6
5. Titus 3:5

—ELVINA M. HALL, 1865

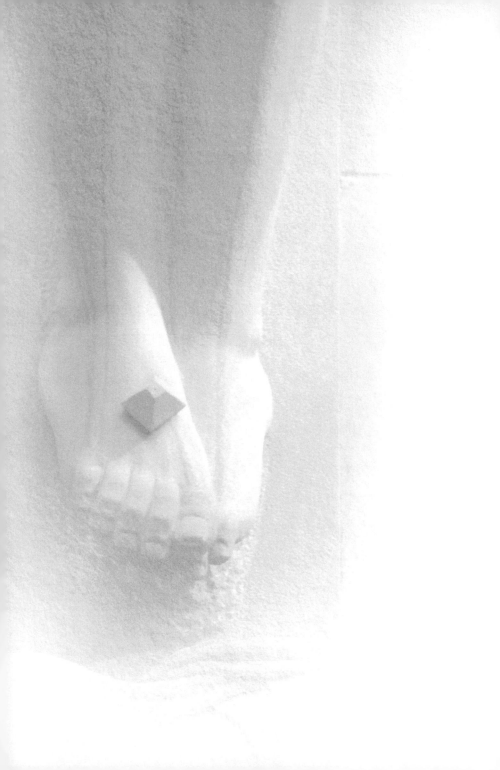

EASTER

Hallelujah, once and for all, Death is defeated! As it gasped its last breath, You tore us from the grip of the grave. It has forever lost its fearsome power over us. And You, our victor, are but the first of many to emerge not only unharmed but transformed!

If this doesn't make us laugh out loud, the truth hasn't dawned on us at all. This is simply the best news a mortal can get: "You're the luckiest person on the planet—you've just won a contest you didn't even enter!" It's not an idea or simply a dogma. It's real. It's now.

You are risen. You are risen indeed!

EASTER SUNDAY

Lord of all life and power, who through the mighty resurrection of your Son overcame the old order of sin and death to make all things new: grant that we, being dead to sin and alive to you in Jesus Christ, may reign with him in glory; to whom with you and the Spirit be praise and honour, glory and might, now and in all eternity. Amen.

THOMAS CRANMER, 1489-1586

PAST AND FUTURE

The Blood of Jesus washes away our past and the Name of Jesus opens up our future.

JESSE DUPLANTIS, 1949-

ARISE, MY SOUL, ARISE!

LEWIS EDSON, 1782

Arise, my soul, arise; shake off thy guilty fears;[1]
The bleeding sacrifice in my behalf appears:
Before the throne my surety stands,
Before the throne my surety stands,
My name is written on His hands.

He ever lives above, for me to intercede;[2]
His all redeeming love, His precious blood, to plead:
His blood atoned for all our race,
His blood atoned for all our race,
And sprinkles now the throne of grace.

Five bleeding wounds He bears; received on Calvary;
They pour effectual prayers; they strongly plead for me:
"Forgive him, O forgive," they cry,
"Forgive him, O forgive," they cry,
"Nor let that ransomed sinner die!"

The Father hears Him pray, His dear anointed One;
He cannot turn away, the presence of His Son;
His Spirit answers to the blood,
His Spirit answers to the blood,
And tells me I am born of God.[3]

My God is reconciled; His pardoning voice I hear;
He owns me for His child; I can no longer fear:
With confidence I now draw nigh,
With confidence I now draw nigh[4]
And "Father, Abba, Father," cry.[5]

1. Isaiah 60:1-3
2. Hebrews 7:25
3. Romans 8:16
4. Hebrews 4:16
5. Romans 8:15

CHARLES WESLEY, 1742

JESUS, I AM RESTING

Jesus, I am resting, resting
In the joy of what Thou art;
I am finding out the greatness
Of Thy loving heart.
Thou hast bid me gaze upon Thee,
And Thy beauty fills my soul,
For by Thy transforming power,
Thou hast made me whole.

O, how great Thy loving kindness,
Vaster, broader than the sea!
O, how marvelous Thy goodness,
Lavished all on me!
Yes, I rest in Thee, Belovèd,
Know what wealth of grace is Thine,
Know Thy certainty of promise,
And have made it mine.

Simply trusting Thee, Lord Jesus,
I behold Thee as Thou art,
And Thy love, so pure, so changeless,
Satisfies my heart;
Satisfies its deepest longings,
Meets, supplies its every need,
Encompasseth me round with blessings
Thine is love indeed!

Ever lift Thy face upon me
As I work and wait for Thee;
Resting 'neath Thy smile, Lord Jesus,
Earth's dark shadows flee.
Brightness of my Father's glory,
Sunshine of my Father's face,
Keep me ever trusting, resting,
Fill me with Thy grace.

—JEAN SOPHIA PIGOTT, 1845-1882

IT IS WELL WITH MY SOUL

PHILIP P. BLISS, 1876

When peace, like a riv - er, at - tend - eth my way,

when sor - rows like sea bil - lows roll; what ev - er my

lot, thou hast taught me to say, It is well, it is well with my soul.

Refrain

It is well with my soul it is well, it is well with my soul.[1]

2. Tho' Satan should buffet, tho' trials should come,
   Let this blest assurance control,
   That Christ hath regarded my helpless estate,[2]
   And hath shed His own blood for my soul.
      Refrain

3. My sin—oh, the bliss of this glorious thought—
   My sin, not in part but the whole
   Is nailed to the cross and I bear it no more.
   Praise the Lord, praise the Lord, O my soul.
      Refrain

4. And, Lord, haste the day when my faith shall be sight,[3]
   The clouds be rolled back as a scroll,
   The trump shall resound and the Lord shall descend.[4]
   Even so—it is well with my soul.
      Refrain

—HORATIO G. SPAFFORD, 1873

1. Ecclesiastes 8:12
2. Romans 5:6
3. 2 Corinthians 5:6-8
4. 1 Thessalonians 4:16

HE HAS DESTROYED DEATH

He has destroyed death by undergoing death.
He has despoiled hell by descending into hell.
Hell was filled with bitterness when it met Thee face to face below;
filled with bitterness, for it was brought to nothing;
filled with bitterness, for it was mocked;
filled with bitterness, for it was overthrown;
filled with bitterness, for it was put in chains.
Hell received a body, and encountered God. It received earth, and
    confronted heaven.
O death, where is your sting?
O hell, where is your victory?

Christ is risen! And you, o death, are annihilated!
Christ is risen! And the evil ones are cast down!
Christ is risen! And the angels rejoice!
Christ is risen! And life is liberated!
Christ is risen! And the tomb is emptied of its dead;
for Christ having risen from the dead,
is become the first-fruits of those who have fallen asleep.

To Him be Glory and Power, now and forever,
and from all ages to all ages.
Amen!

—JOHN CHRYSOSTOM, 347–407

FREEDOM

If I really believed I was free,
   my heart would leap in me for joy.
My face would shine bright as the sun,
   if I really believed I was free.

I'd throw a freedom party and dance around
   like a drunken fool into the late hours of the night.
I would gleefully tell everyone all about my story—
   my captivity, my release, and
      all about Who freed me.

If I really believed I was free,
   I'd smile more and laugh easily.
There simply wouldn't be much space left
   in my heart for the grim,
      if I really believed.

—JOHN RANDALL DENNIS, 1957-

AMAZING GRACE

—AMERICAN, 19TH CENTURY

A - maz - ing grace! How sweet the sound that saved a wretch like me! [1]

once was lost, but now am found; was blind, but now I see.

2. 'Twas grace that taught my
    heart to fear,
   And grace my fears relieved;
   How precious did that grace
    appear
   The hour I first believed! [2]

3. Through many dangers, toils,
    and snares,
   I have already come; [3]
   'Tis grace hath brought me
    safe thus far,
   And grace will lead me home.

4. The Lord has promised good
    to me, [4]
   His Word my hope secures;
   He will my Shield and Portion
    be, [5]
   As long as life endures.

5. Yea, when this flesh and heart
    shall fail,
   And mortal life shall cease,
   I shall possess, within the veil,
   A life of joy and peace.

6. The earth shall soon dissolve
    like snow,
   The sun forbear to shine;
   But God, who called me here
    below,
   Will be forever mine.

7. When we've been there ten
    thousand years,
   Bright shining as the sun, [6]
   We've no less days to sing
    God's praise
   Than when we'd first begun.

1. 1 Timothy 1:15
2. Ephesians 2:4-6
3. 2 Corinthians 11:25-27
4. Romans 8:28
5. Psalm 33:20; 142:5
6. Revelation 22:5

—JOHN NEWTON, 1779

EASTER BEATITUDES

Blessed are they of the Easter Faith,
For theirs is the risen Lord;
For them he lives, and to them he gives
The fountain of life restored.

Blessed are they of the Easter Cheer,
For theirs is the burning heart;
For them the tomb is bereft of gloom,
They walk with their Lord apart.

Blessed are they of the Easter Hope,
For theirs is the open gate;
It swings through the tomb to that other room
Where the Lord and our loved ones wait.

—CLARENCE M. BURKHOLDER, n.d.

SECOND SUNDAY OF EASTER

Almighty Father, you have given your only Son to die for our sins and to rise again for our justification: grant us to put away the leaven of malice and wickedness that we may always serve you in pureness of living and truth, through the merits of your Son Jesus Christ our Lord, who is alive and reigns with you, in the unity of the Spirit, one God, now and for ever. Amen.

—THOMAS CRANMER 1489-1586

CROWN HIM WITH MANY CROWNS

—GEORGE J. ELVEY, 1868

Crown Him with many crowns, the Lamb upon His throne.[1]
Hark! How the heavenly anthem drowns all music but its own.
Awake, my soul, and sing of Him who died for thee,[2]
And hail Him as thy matchless King through all eternity.

Crown Him the Lord of life, who triumphed o'er the grave,
And rose victorious in the strife for those He came to save.
His glories now we sing, Who died, and rose on high,
Who died eternal life to bring, and lives that death may die.[3]

Crown Him the Lord of peace, Whose power a scepter sways
From pole to pole, that wars may cease, and all be prayer and praise.[4]
His reign shall know no end, and round His piercèd feet
Fair flowers of paradise extend their fragrance ever sweet.

Crown Him the Lord of love, behold His hands and side,
Those wounds, yet visible above, in beauty glorified.[5]
No angel in the sky can fully bear that sight,
But downward bends his burning eye at mysteries so bright.[6]

Crown Him the Lord of Heaven, enthroned in worlds above,
Crown Him the King to Whom is given the wondrous name of Love.
Crown Him with many crowns, as thrones before Him fall;[7]
Crown Him, ye kings, with many crowns, for He is King of all.

1. Revelation 7:9-11
2. Psalm 108:1
3. John 3:14-16
4. Hebrews 1:7-9
5. 1 Peter 2:23-25
6. 1 Peter 1:11-13
7. Revelation 4:10

—MATTHEW BRIDGES, 1852

NOT IN VAIN

Hope we not in this life only.
Christ himself has made it plain
None who sleep in Him shall perish,
And our faith is not in vain.
Not in vain our glad hosannas;
Since we follow where He led,
Not in vain our Easter anthem:
"Christ has risen from the dead!"

—ANONYMOUS

THE END OF VAIN RELIGION,
THE BEGINNING OF DELIGHT

"If Christ has not been raised, then our preaching is vain, your faith also is vain" (1 Corinthians 15:14). If Christ has not been raised, we might as well pack it up and go home. We're frankly better off sleeping in rather than going to church. But if He really has been raised, this proclaims the end of all fear. This is the end of striving to be perfect and religious. It is the beginning of reckless delight. Let's not miss any of the fun.

—JOHN RANDALL DENNIS, 1957-

THOU WILT DIRECT OUR PATHS

O Lord, the God of our salvation, thou still watchest over us for good; thou daily renewest to us our lives and thy mercies; and thou hast given us the assurance of thy word that if we commit our affairs to thee, if we acknowledge thee in all our ways, thou wilt direct our paths.

—JOHN WESLEY, 1703-1791

THE FURNACE OF LOVE

O Sacred Heart of Jesus, fountain of eternal life, Your Heart is a glowing furnace of Love. You are my refuge and my sanctuary. O my adorable and loving Savior, consume my heart with the burning fire with which Yours is aflamed. Pour down on my soul those graces which flow from Your love. Let my heart be united with Yours. Let my will be conformed to Yours in all things. May Your Will be the rule of all my desires and actions. Amen.

—SAINT GERTRUDE THE GREAT, 1256-1301

COMMUNION

Here, O my Lord, I see Thee face to face;
here would I touch and handle things unseen;
here grasp with firmer hand eternal grace,
and all my weariness upon Thee lean.[1]

This is the hour of banquet and of song;[2]
This is the heavenly table spread for me;[3]
Here let me feast, and feasting, still prolong
The hallowed hour of fellowship with Thee.

Here would I feed upon the bread of God,
here drink with Thee the royal wine of heaven;
here would I lay aside each earthly load,
here taste afresh the calm of sin forgiven.[4]

Too soon we rise; the symbols disappear;
the feast, though not the love, is past and gone.
The bread and wine remove; but Thou art here,
nearer than ever, still my shield and sun.

Feast after feast thus comes and passes by;
yet, passing, points to the glad feast above,
giving sweet foretaste of the festal joy,
the Lamb's great bridal feast of bliss and love.[5]

1. Matthew 11:28
2. Matthew 22
3. Psalm 23:5
4. Ephesians 1:7-8
5. Revelation 19:7-9

—HORATIUS BONAR, 1855

LIVING BREAD

Almighty God, grant us grace to hear Jesus Christ, the heavenly bread, preached throughout the world, and truly understand him. May all evil, heretical and human doctrines be cut off, while thy word as the living bread be distributed. Amen.

—MARTIN LUTHER, 1483–1546

THIRD SUNDAY OF EASTER

Almighty Father, who in your great mercy gladdened the disciples with the sight of the risen Lord: give us such knowledge of his presence with us, that we may be strengthened and sustained by his risen life and serve you continually in righteousness and truth; through Jesus Christ your Son our Lord, who is alive and reigns with you, in the unity of the Holy Spirit, one God, now and for ever. Amen.

—THOMAS CRANMER, 1489–1586

I WILL SING OF THE MERCIES OF THE LORD

—JAMES H. FILMORE, n.d.

1 will sing of the mer-cies of the Lord for-ev-er. 1 will sing, 1 will

sing. sing of the mer-cies of the Lord.[1] With my mouth will 1 make

known Thy faith-ful-ness, Thy faith-ful-ness, with my mouth will 1 make

known Thy faith-ful-ness to all gen-er-a-tions.[2]

1. Psalm 81:1a
2. Psalm 81:1b

—PHILIP P. BLISS, 1876

A PRAYER FOR GOD'S LIGHT

O Lord, grant us that love which can never die, which will enkindle our lamps but not extinguish them, so that they may shine in us and bring light to others. Most dear Savior, enkindle our lamps that they may shine forever in your temple. May we receive unquench-able light from you so that our darkness will be illuminated and the darkness of the world will be made less. Amen.

—Columba, Abbot of Iona, 521–590

MY REDEEMER LIVES

—Reuben Morgan, 1998

I know He res-cued my soul [2]
My shame He's tak-en a-way [2] His blood has my pain is
cov-ered my sin [1] I be-lieve I be-lieve
healed in His name [3]
I'll raise a ban - ner My Lord has con-quered the grave [4] My Re-
deem - er lives My Re-deem - er lives My Re-
deem - er lives My Re-deem - er lives. [5]

Fine

2. You lift my burden, I'll rise with You;
   I'm dancing on this mountaintop
   to see Your kingdom come.
      Refrain

1. Romans 4:6-8
2. Philippians 1:19-21
3. Isaiah 53:4-6
4. 1 Corinthians 15:55
5. Job 19:25

—Reuben Morgan, 1998

PROCLAIM CHRIST

Almighty God, grant that all preachers may proclaim Christ and thy word with power and blessing everywhere. Grant that all who hear thy word preached may learn to know Christ and amend their ways. Wilt thou also graciously remove from the Church all preaching and teaching which does not honor Christ.

—MARTIN LUTHER, 1483–1546

TEMPORARY THINGS

You will be in heaven two seconds before crying out, "Why did I place so much importance on things that were so temporary? What was I thinking?"

—RICK WARREN, 1954-

WHAT A FRIEND WE HAVE IN JESUS

—Charles C. Converse, 1868

What a friend we have in Je - sus, all our sins and griefs to bear![1]

What a priv - i - lege to car - ry ev - ery-thing to God in prayer!

O what peace we of - ten for - feit, O what need-less pain we bear,

all be-cause we do not car - ry ev - ery-thing to God in prayer.

2. Have we trials and temptations? Is there trouble anywhere?
We should never be discouraged; take it to the Lord in prayer.[2]
Can we find a friend so faithful who will all our sorrows share?
Jesus knows our every weakness; take it to the Lord in prayer.

3. Are we weak and heavy laden, cumbered with a load of care?
Precious Savior, still our refuge, take it to the Lord in prayer.
Do your friends despise, forsake you? Take it to the Lord in prayer!
In His arms He'll take and shield you; you will find a solace there.

4. Blessed Savior, Thou hast promised Thou wilt all our burdens bear.[3]
May we ever, Lord, be bringing all to Thee in earnest prayer.
Soon in glory bright, unclouded there will be no need for prayer.
Rapture, praise, and endless worship will be our sweet portion there.

1. Matthew 11:28
2. James 5:13
3. Jeremiah 31:25

—Joseph Scriven, 1855

TO KNOW CHRIST PERSONALLY

Yes, all things I once thought were so important are gone from my life. Compared to the high privilege of knowing Jesus Christ as my Master, firsthand, everything I once thought I had going for me is insignificant—dog dung. I've dumped it all in the trash so that I can embrace Christ and be embraced by Him. I don't want some petty inferior brand of righteousness that comes from keeping a list of rules when I could get the robust kind that comes from trusting Christ— God's righteousness. I gave up all that inferior stuff so I could know Christ personally, experience His resurrection power, be a partner in His suffering, and go all the way with Him to death itself.

—EUGENE PETERSON, 1932-
  (FROM PHILIPPIANS 3:7-10 *THE MESSAGE*)

THE GREATEST CHRISTIAN

The greatest Christian is not the one who has achieved the most but rather the one who has received the most.

—JIM CYMBALA, 1948-

GENUINE CHANGE

There is little hope for genuine change in one who is without remorse, without the anguish of regret.

—DALLAS WILLARD, 1935-

FOURTH SUNDAY OF EASTER

Almighty God, whose Son Jesus Christ is the resurrection and the life: raise us, who trust in him, from the death of sin to the life of righteousness, that we may seek things which are above, where he reigns with you in the unity of the Spirit, one God, now and forever. Amen.

—THOMAS CRANMER, 1489–1586

BEAUTIFUL SAVIOR

—Schlesische Volkslieder, 1842

Beau - ti - ful Sav - ior, King of cre - a - tion,

Son of God and Son of man! Tru - ly I'd love - Thee,

tru - ly I'd serve - Thee, Light of my soul, my joy, my crown.

2. Fair are the meadows, fair are the woodlands,
   Robed in flowers of blooming spring;
   Jesus is fairer, Jesus is purer,
   He makes our sorrowing spirit sing.[1]

3. Fair is the sunshine, fair is the moonlight,
   Bright the sparkling stars on high;
   Jesus shines brighter, Jesus shines purer
   Than all the angels in the sky.

4. Beautiful Savior, Lord of the nations,
   Son of God and Son of Man![2]
   Glory and honor, praise, adoration
   Now and forevermore be Thine![3]

1. Psalm 21:6
2. Revelation 1:12–14
3. Psalm 45:2; Revelation 22:4–6

—Münster Gesangbuch, 1677

CENTER STAGE

In the New Testament, Jesus upstages everyone else. He is not only the center of the gospel, he is the whole gospel. He is the good news. The four evangelists never focus on another personality. Fringe people stay on the fringe, marginal men and women stay on the margin. No one else is allowed to take center stage.

—BRENNAN MANNING, 1939-

GOOD NIGHT PRAYER

Good night, dear Jesus, Your presence I adore.
Grant me to love You more and more.
Do keep me near You that I may holy be.
Dear Gentle Jesus, Good night.
Heart of my Savior, protect me in sleep,
my heart forever in Your love keep.
Bless me, dear Savior, and keep me in Your sight.
Dear Gentle Jesus, Good night.

—THE MONKS OF ADORATION, n.d.

JOYFUL, JOYFUL WE ADORE THEE

—LUDWIG VAN BEETHOVEN, 1868

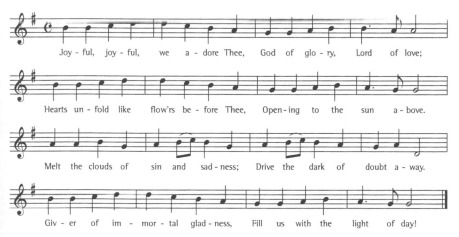

Joy - ful, joy - ful, we a - dore Thee, God of glo - ry, Lord of love;

Hearts un - fold like flow'rs be - fore Thee, Open - ing to the sun a - bove.

Melt the clouds of sin and sad - ness; Drive the dark of doubt a - way.

Giv - er of im - mor - tal glad - ness, Fill us with the light of day!

2. All Thy works with joy surround Thee, earth and heaven reflect Thy rays,[1]
   Stars and angels sing around Thee, center of unbroken praise.
   Field and forest, vale and mountain, flowery meadow, flashing sea,
   Singing bird and flowing fountain call us to rejoice in Thee.[2]

3. Thou art giving and forgiving, ever blessing, ever blessed,
   Wellspring of the joy of living, ocean depth of happy rest!
   Thou our Father, Christ our Brother, all who live in love are Thine;
   Teach us how to love each other, lift us to the joy divine.

4. Mortals, join the happy chorus, which the morning stars began;
   Father love is reigning o'er us, brother love binds man to man.
   Ever singing, march we onward, victors in the midst of strife,
   Joyful music leads us sunward in the triumph song of life.[3]

1. Psalm 139:14
2. Psalm 150:6
3. Psalm 63:7

—HENRY VAN DYKE, 1907

JESU, JOY OF MAN'S DESIRING

—Johan Schop, 1642

Je - su, joy of man's de - sir - ing, Ho - ly wis - dom, Love most bright[1] Drawn by Thee, our souls as - pir - ing Soar to un - cre - a - ted light.[2] Word of God, our flesh that fash - ion'd[3] With the fire of life im - pas - sion'd. Striv - ing still to Truth un - known, Soar - ing, dy - ing, round Thy throne.

2. Through the way where hope is guiding,
   Hark, what peaceful music rings;
   Where the flock, in Thee confiding,
   Drink of joy from deathless springs.
   Theirs is beauty's fairest pleasure;
   Theirs is wisdom's holiest treasure.
   Thou dost ever lead Thine own
   In the love of joys unknown.

1. Revelation 7:12
2. 1 Peter 2:9
3. John 1:1

—Martin Janus, 1661

150

ON OBEDIENCE

Don't you think Christ delights in our glad responses when we rejoice to obey Him? Let me be clear that God honors obedience even where we're kicking and screaming. Can you imagine how blessed He is when we're eager to do His will?

—BETH MOORE, 1957–

MAY GOD THE FATHER BLESS US

May God the Father bless us;
may Christ take care of us;
the Holy Ghost enlighten us all the days of our life.
The Lord be our defender and keeper of body and soul,
both now and for ever, to the ages of ages.

—ÆTHELWOLD, C. 908–984

DEVOTION

God of my end, it is my greatest, noblest pleasure to be acquainted with Thee and with my rational, immortal soul; it is sweet and entertaining to look into my being when all my powers and passions are united and engaged in pursuit of Thee, when my soul longs and passionately breathes after conformity to Thee and the full enjoyment of Thee; no hours pass away with so much pleasure as those spent in communion with Thee and with my heart.

—PURITAN PRAYERS, C. 1700

ALL IN ALL

Do you fear wrath? Christ can deliver you from the wrath to come. Do you feel the curse of a broken law? Christ can redeem you from the curse of the law. Do you feel far away? Christ has suffered, to bring you nigh to God. Do you feel unclean? Christ's blood can cleanse all sin away. Do you feel imperfect? You shall be complete in Christ. Do you feel as if you were nothing? Christ shall be "all in all" to your soul.

—J. C. RYLE, 1816-1900

FIFTH SUNDAY OF EASTER

Almighty God, who through your only begotten Son Jesus Christ have overcome death and opened the gate of everlasting life: grant that, as by your grace going before us you put into our minds good desires, so by your continual help we may bring them to good effect; through Jesus Christ our risen Lord, who is alive and reigns with you, in the unity of the Spirit, one God, now and for ever. Amen.

—THOMAS CRANMER, 1489-1586

AN UNDIVIDED HEART

*O divine Redeemer, out of whose inex-
haustible fullness I would daily draw a rich
supply of grace into my needy soul, be
pleased to impart unto me an undivided
heart; that to please You, may be my greatest
happiness, and to promote Your glory my
highest honor. Preserve me from false
motives, from a double mind, and a divided
heart. Keep me entirely to Yourself, and
enable me to crucify every lust which would
tempt my heart from You. Enable me by Your
grace to walk in one uniform path of holy,
childlike obedience. When tempted to turn
aside to the right hand or to the left, may I
keep steadily on Your way, until brought
before Your throne, I see Your face, behold
Your smile, and fall in ecstasy at Your feet,
lost in wonder, love, and praise.*

—THOMAS READE, 1841-1909

MY JESUS, I LOVE THEE

—ADONIRAM J. GORDON, 1876

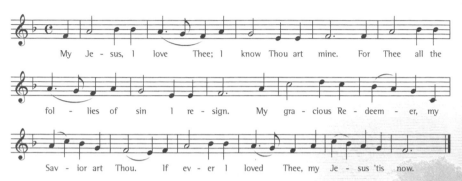

My Je - sus, I love Thee; I know Thou art mine. For Thee all the fol - lies of sin I re - sign. My gra - cious Re - deem - er, my Sav - ior art Thou. If ev - er I loved Thee, my Je - sus 'tis now.

2. I love Thee because Thou hast first lovèd me,[1]
   And purchased my pardon on Calvary's tree.[2]
   I love Thee for wearing the thorns on Thy brow;[3]
   If ever I loved Thee, my Jesus, 'tis now.

3. I'll love Thee in life, I will love Thee in death,
   And praise Thee as long as Thou lendest me breath;
   And say when the death dew lies cold on my brow,
   If ever I loved Thee, my Jesus, 'tis now.

4. In mansions of glory and endless delight,[4]
   I'll ever adore Thee in heaven so bright;
   I'll sing with the glittering crown on my brow;[5]
   If ever I loved Thee, my Jesus, 'tis now.

1. 1 John 4:19
2. Acts 20:28
3. Mark 15:17
4. John 14:2
5. Revelation 3:11

—WILLIAM R. FEATHERSTON, 1864

PARTICIPATING IN GOD'S PLAN

Participating in God's plan involves more than an initial response. Every day includes new opportunities to cooperate with his purposes. We must also follow when God leads us in unexpected directions.

—CHIP INGRAM, n.d.

SALVATION BY GRACE

Remember this; or you may fall into error by fixing your minds so much upon the faith which is the channel of salvation as to forget the grace which is the fountain and source even of faith itself. Faith is the work of God's grace in us. "No man comes to Me," says Jesus, "except the Father who sent Me draws him. . . ." Grace is the first and last moving cause of salvation; and faith, essential as it is, is only an important part of the machinery which grace employs. We are saved "through faith," but salvation is "by grace."

—CHARLES SPURGEON, 1834–1892

HOW FIRM A FOUNDATION

—JOHANN M. HAYDN, n.d.

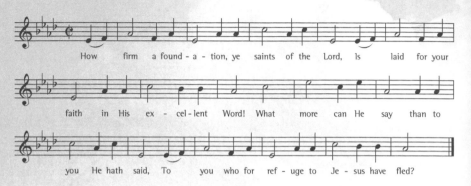

How firm a found-a-tion, ye saints of the Lord, Is laid for your faith in His ex-cel-lent Word! What more can He say than to you He hath said, To you who for ref-uge to Je-sus have fled?

2. In every condition, in sickness, in health;
   In poverty's vale, or abounding in wealth;
   At home and abroad, on the land, on the sea,
   As thy days may demand, shall thy strength ever be.

3. Fear not, I am with thee, O be not dismayed,
   For I am thy God, I will still give thee aid;
   I'll strengthen thee, help thee, and cause thee to stand
   Upheld by My gracious, omnipotent hand.[1]

4. When through the deep waters I call thee to go,
   The rivers of sorrow shall not overflow;
   For I will be with thee, thy trials to bless,
   And sanctify to thee thy deepest distress.

5. When through fiery trials thy pathway shall lie,[2]
   My grace all-sufficient shall be thy supply;[3]
   The flame shall not hurt thee; I only design[4]
   Thy dross to consume, and thy gold to refine.[5]

6. Even down to old age all My people shall prove
   My sovereign, eternal, unchangeable love;
   And when hoary hairs shall their temples adorn,
   Like lambs they shall still in My bosom be borne.

7. The soul that on Jesus has leaned for repose,
   I will not, I will not desert to its foes;[6]
   That soul, though all hell should endeavor to shake,
   I'll never, no never, no never forsake.[7]

1. Isaiah 41:10
2. 1 Peter 4:12
3. 2 Corinthians 12:9
4. Isaiah 43:1-2
5. Isaiah 1:25
6. Hebrews 6:18
7. 2 Timothy 2:19

—JOHN RIPPON, 1787

PROPHET, PRIEST, AND KING

It pleased God, in his eternal purpose, to choose and ordain the Lord Jesus, his only begotten Son, to be the Mediator between God and men, the prophet, priest, and king; the head and Savior of the Church, the heir of all things, and judge of the world; unto whom he did, from all eternity, give a people to be his seed, and to be by him in time redeemed, called, justified, sanctified, and glorified. The Son of God, the second Person in the Trinity, being very and eternal God, of one substance, and equal with the Father, did, when the fullness of time was come, take upon himself man's nature, with all the essential properties and common infirmities thereof, yet without sin: being conceived by the power of the Holy Ghost, in the womb of the Virgin Mary, of her substance. So that two whole, perfect, and distinct natures, the Godhead and the manhood, were inseparably joined together in one person, without conversion, composition, or confusion. Which person is very God and very man, yet one Christ, the only Mediator between God and man.

—WESTMINSTER CONFESSION OF FAITH, 1647

JESUS SHALL REIGN

—JOHN HATTON, 1793

Je - sus shall reign wher - e'er the sun Does his suc - ces - sive

jour - neys run; His king-dom stretch from shore to shore,

Till moons shall wax and wane no more.[1]

2. To Him shall endless prayer be made,
   And praises throng to crown His head;
   His name like sweet perfume shall rise
   With every morning sacrifice.

3. People and realms of every tongue
   Dwell on His love with sweetest song;
   And infant voices shall proclaim
   Their early blessings on His name.[2]

4. Blessings abound where'er He reigns;
   The prisoner leaps to lose his chains;
   The weary find eternal rest,
   And all the sons of want are blessed.

5. Where He displays His healing power,
   Death and the curse are known
            no more:[3]
   In Him the tribes of Adam boast
   More blessings than their father lost.

6. Let every creature rise and bring
   Peculiar honors to our King;
   Angels descend with songs again,
   And earth repeat the loud amen![4]

7. The saints shall flourish in His days,
   Dressed in the robes of joy and praise;
   Peace, like a river, from His throne
   Shall flow to nations yet unknown.

1. Revelation 11:15
2. Daniel 4:3
3. Acts 10:38
4. Psalm 72:19

—ISAAC WATTS, 1719

ON FAITH IN THE RESURRECTION

God our Redeemer, you have saved us from the power of darkness and brought us into the kingdom of your Son. You have granted that by his death he has called us to life: and so by his continual presence raises us to eternal joy. This we ask through Jesus Christ, your Son and our Lord, who is alive with you, in the unity of the Spirit, one God, now and for ever.

—GEORGE E. LADD, 1911–1982

PRECIOUS BLOOD

Precious Blood,
Ocean of Divine Mercy:
Flow upon us!

Precious Blood,
Most pure Offering:
Procure us every Grace!

Precious Blood,
Hope and Refuge of sinners:
Atone for us!

Precious Blood,
Delight of holy souls:
Draw us! Amen.

—CATHERINE OF SIENA, 1347–1380

JESUS, NAME ABOVE ALL NAMES

—Patricia Cain and Naida Hearn, 1974

Je - sus, name a-bove all names,[1] beau-ti-ful Sav - ior, glo-ri-ous Lord. Em - man - u - el, God is with us,[2] bless-ed Re - deem - er, liv - ing Word.[3]

1. Philippians 2:9-11
2. Matthew 1:23
3. John 1:1

—Patricia Cain and Naida Hearn, 1974

SIXTH SUNDAY OF EASTER

God our redeemer, you have delivered us from the power of darkness and brought us into the kingdom of your Son: grant, that as by his death he has recalled us to life, so by his continual presence in us he may raise us to eternal joy, through Jesus Christ your Son our Lord, who is alive and reigns with you, in the unity of the Spirit, one God, now and for ever. Amen.

—Thomas Cranmer, 1489-1586

O WORSHIP THE KING

—JOHANN M. HAYDN, n.d.

O wor-ship the King, all glo-rious a-bove, O grate-ful-ly sing God's pow-er and God's love; our Shield and De-fend-er the An-cient of days, pa-vil-ioned in splen-dor and gird-ed with praise.

2. O tell of His might, O sing of His grace,
   Whose robe is the light, whose canopy space.
   His chariots of wrath the deep thunderclouds form,
   And dark is His path on the wings of the storm.

3. Thy bountiful care what tongue can recite?
   It breathes in the air, it shines in the light;
   It streams from the hills, it descends to the plain,
   And sweetly distills in the dew and the rain.

4. Frail children of dust, and feeble as frail,
   In Thee do we trust, nor find Thee to fail;
   Thy mercies how tender, how firm to the end,
   Our Maker, Defender, Redeemer, and Friend.

—ROBERT GRANT, 1833

STRIKING A BALANCE

Knowing God without knowing our own wretchedness makes for PRIDE. Knowing our own wretchedness without knowing God makes for DESPAIR. Knowing JESUS CHRIST strikes the balance because he shows us both God and our own wretchedness.

—Blaise Pascal, 1623-1662

JOY FOREVER AND EVER

It will take an infinite number of ages for God to be done glorifying the wealth of his grace to us—which is to say he will never be done. And our joy will increase forever and ever. Boredom is absolutely excluded in the presence of an infinitely glorious God.

—John Piper, 1946-

WHO IS MY GOD?

In His eyes there is no anger at my weakness. There is not a harsh word on His lips for my unbelief. He does not wish to break me or harm me. He does not sigh at my shortcomings. The Lord my God only holds me closer and whispers poems and lyrics to comfort my soul. He prepares a feast in my honor, and He has moved my seat next to His. He lets me eat until I am full and laughing. How great is my God! Always, I will declare him King. Forever I will love Him.

—John Wesley Dennis III, 1987-

ONE DEGREE

Much of the time the devil ensnares us one small lie at a time. If he told us a whopping lie, we'd recognize him for the liar he is. He chooses to tell us small lies that are just one degree away from the truth.

—CHARLES F. STANLEY, 1932-

A PRAYER FOR GUIDANCE

O creator past all telling, You have appointed from the treasures of your wisdom the hierarchies of angels, disposing them in wondrous order above the bright heavens, and have so beautifully set out all parts of the universe.

You we call the true fount of wisdom and the noble origin of all things. Be pleased to shed on the darkness of mind in which I was born, the twofold beam of your light and warmth to dispel my ignorance and sin.

You make eloquent the tongues of children. Then instruct my speech and touch my lips with graciousness. Make me keen to understand, quick to learn, able to remember; make me delicate to interpret and ready to speak.

Guide my going in and going forward, lead home my going forth. You are true God and true man, and live for ever and ever.

—THOMAS AQUINAS, 1225-1274

ALL HAIL THE POWER OF JESUS' NAME

—OLIVER HOLDEN, 1793

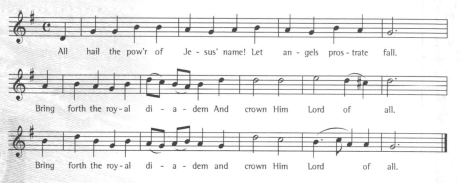

All hail the pow'r of Je - sus' name! Let an - gels pros - trate fall.

Bring forth the roy - al di - a - dem And crown Him Lord of all.

Bring forth the roy - al di - a - dem and crown Him Lord of all.

2. Ye seed of Israel's chosen race, ye ransomed from the fall,
   Hail Him Who saves you by His grace, and crown Him Lord of all.
   Hail Him Who saves you by His grace, and crown Him Lord of all.

3. Let every tribe and every tongue before Him prostrate fall
   And shout in universal song the crownèd Lord of all.
   And shout in universal song the crownèd Lord of all.

4. Oh, that with yonder sacred throng we at His feet may fall,
   Join in the everlasting song, and crown Him Lord of all,
   Join in the everlasting song, and crown Him Lord of all!

—EDWARD PERRONET, 1779

THE TASTE OF JOY

As soon as we do totally surrender, abandoning ourselves to Jesus, the Holy Spirit gives us a taste of His joy. The ultimate goal of self-sacrifice is to lay down our lives for our Friend (see John 15:13-14). When the Holy Spirit comes into our lives, our greatest desire is to lay down our lives for Jesus. Yet the thought of self-sacrifice never even crosses our minds, because sacrifice is the Holy Spirit's ultimate expression of love.

—OSWALD CHAMBERS, 1874-1917

MORE PRECIOUS THAN SILVER

—LYNN DESHAZO, 1982

Lord, you are more pre-cious than sil-ver. Lord, you are more cost-ly than gold. Lord, you are more beau-ti-ful than dia-monds, and noth-ing I de-sire com-pares with you.

2. Child, you are more precious than silver;
   Child, you are more costly than gold;
   Child, you are more beautiful than diamonds,
   And nothing I desire compares with you.

3. Lord, Your love is wider than the oceans;
   Lord, Your love is deeper than the seas;
   Lord, Your love encompasses the nations,
   And nothing I want more inside of me.

—LYNN DESHAZO, 1982

SEVENTH SUNDAY OF EASTER

O God, the King of glory, you have raised your only Son Jesus Christ triumphantly to your kingdom in heaven. Do not leave us comfortless, but send your Spirit to strengthen us and raise us also to heaven, where our Savior lives and reigns with you in the unity of the same Spirit, one God, now and for ever.

—THOMAS CRANMER, 1489-1586

TUNE YOUR INSTRUMENT FIRST

Do not have your concert first, and then tune your instrument afterwards. Begin the day with the Word of God and prayer, and get first of all into harmony with Him.

—HUDSON TAYLOR, 1832-1905

HOW TO WALK WITH GOD

Approach the Scriptures not so much as a manual of Christian prin-
ciples but as the testimony of God's friends on what it means to walk
with him through a thousand different episodes. When you are at war,
when you are in love, when you have sinned, when you have been
given a great gift—this is how you walk with God.

—JOHN ELDREDGE, 1960-

PREACH THE HEART OF THE LOVING LAMB

Our method of proclaiming salvation is this: to point out to every
heart the loving Lamb, who died for us, and although He was the Son
of God, offered Himself for our sins...by the preaching of His blood,
and of His love unto death, even the death of the cross, never, either
in discourse or in argument, to digress even for a quarter of an hour
from the loving Lamb: to name no virtue except in Him, and from
Him and on His account—to preach no commandment except faith in
Him; no other justification but that He atoned for us; no other sanctification but the privilege to sin no more; no other happiness but to
be near Him, to think of Him and do His pleasure; no other self-
denial but to be deprived of Him and His blessings; no other calamity
but to displease Him; no other life but in Him.

—COUNT ZINZENDORF, 1700-1760

NOTHING BUT THE BLOOD OF JESUS

—ROBERT LOWRY, 1876

What can wash a - way my sin? Noth-ing but the blood of Je - sus.

What can make me whole a-gain? Noth-ing but the blood of Je - sus.[1]

Refrain

O pre-cious is the flow[2] That makes me white as snow.[3] No oth - er

fount I know — noth - ing but the blood of Je - sus.

2. For my pardon, this I see,
   Nothing but the blood of Jesus;[4]
   For my cleansing, this my plea,[5]
   Nothing but the blood of Jesus.
   Refrain

3. Nothing can for sin atone,
   Nothing but the blood of Jesus;
   Naught of good that I have done,
   Nothing but the blood of Jesus.
   Refrain

4. This is all my hope and peace,
   Nothing but the blood of Jesus;
   This is all my righteousness,
   Nothing but the blood of Jesus.
   Refrain

5. Now by this I'll overcome—
   Nothing but the blood of Jesus,
   Now by this I'll reach my home—
   Nothing but the blood of Jesus.
   Refrain

6. Glory! Glory! This I sing—
   Nothing but the blood of Jesus,
   All my praise for this I bring—
   Nothing but the blood of Jesus.
   Refrain

7. What can wash away my sin?
   Nothing but the blood of Jesus;
   What can make me whole again?
   Nothing but the blood of Jesus.

1. 1 John 1:7
2. John 19:34
3. Isaiah 1:17-19
4. Romans 5:8-9
5. Titus 3:5

—ROBERT LOWRY, 1876

MY FATHER INCLINED HIMSELF TO ME

I myself, for instance, am not especially gifted, and am shy by nature, but my gracious and merciful God and Father inclined Himself to me, and when I was weak in faith He strengthened me while I was still young. He taught me in my helplessness to rest on Him, and to pray even about little things in which another might have felt able to help himself.

—Hudson Taylor, 1832–1905

LORD, ALL MY HEART IS FIXED ON THEE

—Johann S. Bach, 1729

Lord, all my heart is fixed on Thee, I pray Thee, be not far from me,

With ten-der grace up-hold me The whole wide world de-lights me not,[1]

Of heav'n or earth, Lord, ask I not, If but Thy love en-fold me.

Yea, though my heart be like to break, Thou art my trust that nought can shake,

My Por-tion and my hid-den joy,[2] Whose cross could all my bonds de-stroy;

Lord Je-sus Christ! My God and Lord! My God and Lord! For-sake me not who trust Thy Word!

1. James 4:4
2. 2 Corinthians 4:6-8

—Martin Schalling, 1567

PENTECOST

Now are the days of prayers and promises fulfilled! Today is the day of salvation. This is the moment.

True to Your promise, You have not left us as orphans. Your prayer was answered: The Father sent the Helper with a roar and fire. And He did not reserve the Helper for the pious or powerful. He is poured out on all flesh without discrimination—sons and daughters, old and young, male and female, kings and servants, you and me. He walks alongside. He teaches. He brings Christ's words to our remembrance. And He is with us forever! Because He is here, these are also the days of revelation and power.

O Helper, let us not neglect You. Let us never backslide into a religion of law and dogma. Without Your presence and person, our days would only be filled with rules and impotence. We need what You have. We want who You are.

Come, Holy Spirit!

FIRST SUNDAY OF PENTECOST

O Almighty and most merciful God, of your bountiful goodness keep us, we ask, from all things that may hurt us, that we, being ready both in body and soul, may with free hearts accomplish those things which belong to your purpose, through Jesus Christ our Lord, who lives and reigns with you and the Spirit, one God, now and for ever. Amen.

—THOMAS CRANMER, 1489–1556

ALLELUIA! SING TO JESUS!

—ROWLAND H. PRICHARD, 1830

Al - le - lu - ia! Sing to Je - sus! His the scep - ter, His the throne.[1]

Al - le - lu - ia! His the tri - umph, His the vic - to - ry a - lone.

Hark! the songs of peace-ful Zi - on thun - der like a might - y flood:[2]

"Je - sus out of ev - 'ry na - tion has re - deemed us by His blood."

2. Alleluia! not as orphans are we left in sorrow now;[3]
   Alleluia! He is near us, faith believes, nor questions how;
   Though the cloud from sight received Him when the forty days
       were o'er,
   Shall our hearts forget His promise "I am with you evermore"?

3. Alleluia! bread of heaven, here on earth our food and stay!
   Alleluia! here the sinful flee to thee from day to day.
   Intercessor, Friend of sinners, earth's Redeemer, plead for me
   Where the songs of all the sinless sweep across the crystal sea.[4]

1. Hebrews 1:8
2. Colossians 3:16
3. John 14:18
4. Revelation 4:5-7

—WILLIAM C. DIX, 1867

BREATHE ON ME, BREATH OF GOD

—ROBERT JACKSON, 1888

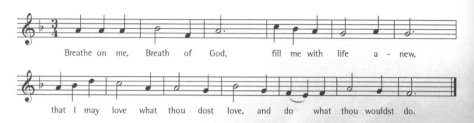

Breathe on me, Breath of God, fill me with life a - new,

that I may love what thou dost love, and do what thou wouldst do.

2. Breathe on me, breath of God,
   Until my heart is pure,
   Until with thee I will one will,
   To do and to endure.

3. Breathe on me, breath of God,
   Blend all my soul with thine,
   Until this earthly part of me
   Glows with thy fire divine.

4. Breathe on me, breath of God,
   So shall I never die,
   But live with thee the perfect life
   Of thine eternity.

—EDWIN HATCH, 1878

THE MOST THRILLING, EXCITING ADVENTURE

If we could but show the world that being committed to Christ is no tame, humdrum, sheltered monotony, but the most thrilling, exciting adventure the human spirit could ever know, those who have been standing outside the church and looking askance at Christ would come crowding in to pay allegiance, and we might well expect the greatest revival since Pentecost.

—DR. JAMES STEWART, 1910-1975

HE LEADETH ME

—William B. Bradbury, 1864

He lead-eth me! O bless-ed tho't! O words with heav'n-ly com-fort fraught!
What-e'er I do, wher-e'er I be, still 'tis God's hand that lead-eth me.[1]

Refrain

He lead-eth me; He lead-eth me. By His own hand He lead-eth me.
His faith-ful fol-l'wer I would be, For by His hand He lead-eth me.

2. Sometimes mid scenes of deepest gloom,
   Sometimes where Eden's bowers bloom,
   By waters still, over troubled sea,[2]
   Still 'tis His hand that leadeth me.[3]

   Refrain

3. Lord, I would place my hand in Thine,
   Nor ever murmur nor repine;
   Content, whatever lot I see,
   Since 'tis my God that leadeth me.

   Refrain

1. Psalm 23:3
2. Isaiah 43:2
3. Exodus 15:13

4. And when my task on earth is done,
   When by Thy grace the vict'ry's won,
   E'en death's cold wave I will not flee,
   Since God through Jordan leadeth me.

   Refrain

—Joseph H. Gilmore, 1862

180

OUR CALLING

Our calling is to surrender to God. Think of the pitfalls we could avoid if we were more abandoned to God than to a particular type of service.

—BETH MOORE, 1957–

ALL OF THE CHRISTIAN RELIGION

All the world religions have been based on human striving to persuade a deity to acknowledge or accept us—the sacrifices, the pains to be better, the self-abasement, or acts of contrition. All of humankind strives on and on like this, but for the followers of Jesus. What He requires is an entirely different matter: "Rest." "Seek." "Ask!" "Knock." "Receive!" "Follow." All of the Christian faith is based on believing Christ has already done everything, and God accepts—even likes—you. If there's any performance it's based on "Have you asked enough?" "Do you know how to receive graciously?" "Can you just relax and learn to trust enough to follow?" Now, that's an easy yoke...that's a light burden! This is a religion even I can practice. And this is a God I'd like to get to know.

—JOHN RANDALL DENNIS, 1957–

MISSING HEAVEN

Hell is not an "oops!" or a slip. One does not miss heaven by a hair, but by constant effort to avoid and escape God.

—DALLAS WILLARD, 1935–

HIDING FROM GOD

Dear God, thank you that no matter where I am, what condition I am in, or what I have done or have failed to do, you know exactly where I am and what condition I am in. Thank you, too, that you are pursuing me not to punish me, but because you want me to come to you for forgiveness, healing, and wholeness. Help me to stop hiding and stop running except to run to your open, loving, and forgiving arms. Thank you for hearing and answering my prayer. Gratefully, in Jesus' name. Amen.

—RICHARD INNES, n.d.

HE WHO BEGAN A GOOD WORK IN YOU

If the struggle you're facing is slowly replacing your hope with despair,
Or the process is long and you're losing your song in the night,
You can be sure that the Lord has His hand on you.
Safe and secure, He will never abandon you.
You are His treasure and He finds His pleasure in you.

—JON MOHR, 1955–

PASS ME NOT

—W. Howard Doane, 1870

Pass me not, O gen-tle Sav-ior, hear my hum-ble cry; while on oth-ers thou art call-ing,

Refrain

do not pass me by.[1] Sav - ior, Sav - ior, hear my hum-ble cry;

while on oth-ers thou art call - ing do not pass me by.

2. Let me at thy throne of mercy[2]
   Find a sweet relief,
   Kneeling there in deep contrition;
   Help my unbelief.[3]
   > *Refrain*

3. Trusting only in thy merit,
   Would I seek thy face;
   Heal my wounded, broken spirit,
   Save me by thy grace.[4]
   > *Refrain*

4. Thou the Spring of all my comfort,
   More than life to me,
   Whom have I on earth beside thee?
   Whom in Heav'n but thee?[5]
   > *Refrain*

—Fanny J. Crosby, 1868

1. Luke 19:3-4
2. Titus 3:5
3. Mark 9:24
4. Romans 11:6
5. Psalm 73:24-26

183

HOLY SPIRIT, RAIN DOWN

—Russell Fragar, 1997

1. 1 Corinthians 2:8-10

—Russell Fragar, 1997

FILL US!

Let us cry out to our Father to so fill us with His Spirit that our lives brim over, spilling His life and joy like refreshing rains on a tired and cynical planet.

—VERNON GROUNDS, 1914–

SECOND SUNDAY OF PENTECOST

Grant, O Lord, that the course of this world may be peaceably governed by your providence, and that your Church may joyfully serve you in confidence and serenity; through Jesus Christ our Lord, who lives and reign with you and the Spirit, one God, for ever and ever. Amen.

—THOMAS CRANMER, 1489–1556

NOTHING LESS THAN PERFECT

"Make no mistake," He says, "if you let Me, I will make you perfect. The moment you put yourself in My hands, that is what you are in for. Nothing less, or other, than that. You have free will, and if you choose, you can push Me away. But if you do not push Me away, understand that I am going to see this job through. Whatever suffering it may cost you in your earthly life...whatever it costs Me, I will never rest, nor let you rest, until you are literally perfect—until My Father can say without reservation that He is well pleased with you, as He said He was well pleased with Me. This I can do and will do. But I will not do anything less."

—C. S. LEWIS, 1898-1963

BEHOLDING AND GROWING

We are predestined to be conformed to your image. When we tasted the kindness of the Lord through You, we were made new creatures. You implanted us with your DNA. Tiny acorns, destined to become mighty oaks. As we behold You we are changed until we are full-grown into your image. Thanks to You there is no striving—only beholding and growing.

JOHN RANDALL DENNIS, 1957-

JUST AS I AM

—William B. Bradbury, 1849

Just as I am, with-out one plea, but that thy blood was
shed for me, and that thou bidst me come to thee,

Refrain

O Lamb of God, I come, I come.

2. Just as I am, and waiting not
To rid my soul of one dark blot,
To thee whose blood can cleanse
each spot,
O Lamb of God, I come, I come.

3. Just as I am, though tossed about
With many a conflict, many a
doubt,
Fightings within, and fears without,
O Lamb of God, I come, I come.

4. Just as I am, poor, wretched, blind;[1]
Sight, riches, healing of the mind,
Yea, all I need in thee to find,
O Lamb of God, I come, I come.

5. Just as I am, thou wilt receive,
Wilt welcome, pardon, cleanse,
relieve;[2]
Because thy promise I believe,
O Lamb of God, I come, I come.

6. Just as I am, thy love unknown
Hath broken every barrier down;
Now to be thine, yea, thine
alone,
O Lamb of God, I come, I come.

7. Just as I am, of that free love
The breadth, length, depth, and
height to prove,
Here for a season, then above,
O Lamb of God, I come, I come!

1. Revelation 3:16-18
2. 1 John 1:7

—Charlotte Elliott, 1836

187

TAKE MY LIFE

—HENRY A. C. MALAN, 1827

Take my life and let it be con-se-cra-ted Lord, to thee.[1]

Take my mo-ments and my days; let them flow with cease-less praise.

Take my hands, and let them move at the im-pulse of thy love.

Take my feet, and let them be swift and beau-ti-ful for thee.[2]

2. Take my voice, and let me sing always, only, for my King.
Take my lips, and let them be filled with messages from thee.
Take my silver and my gold; not a mite would I withhold.[3]
Take my intellect, and use every power as thou shalt choose.[4]

3. Take my will, and make it thine; it shall be no longer mine.
Take my heart, it is thine own; it shall be thy royal throne.
Take my love, my Lord, I pour at thy feet its treasure store.
Take myself, and I will be ever, only, all for thee.

1. Romans 12:1
2. Isaiah 52:7
3. 1 Peter 1:17-19
4. Jeremiah 18:6

—FRANCIS R. HAVERGAL, 1874

NO LONGER DIVIDED

What God asks is a will which will no longer be divided between him and any creature, a will pliant in his hands, which neither desires anything, nor refuses anything, which wants without reservation everything which he wants, and which never, under any pretext, wants anything which he does not want.

—FRANÇOIS DE FENELON, 1651-1715

O GOD, THANK YOU

O God, I thank you that you loved me because I am one who is of the world. O God, thank You. You loved me so much that You gave me Your only begotten Son. I thank You, O God, that You so loved me and gave Your only begotten Son to me, so that by believing in Him I would not perish but would have eternal life.

—WITNESS LEE, 1905-1997

PRAYER TO THE HOLY SPIRIT

Breathe in me, O Holy Spirit, that my thoughts may all be holy. Act in me, O Holy Spirit, that my work, too, may be holy. Draw my heart, O Holy Spirit, that I love but what is holy. Strengthen me, O Holy Spirit, to defend all that is holy. Guard me, then, O Holy Spirit, that I always may be holy. Amen.

—AUGUSTINE OF HIPPO, 354–430

THE OTHER VIEW

The real problem of the Christian life comes the very moment you wake up each morning. All your wishes and hopes for the day rush at you like wild animals. And the first job each morning consists simply in shoving them all back; in listening to that other voice, taking that other view, letting that other, larger, stronger, quieter life come flowing in. And so on, all day. Standing back from all your natural fussings and frettings; coming in out of the wind.

—C. S. LEWIS, 1898–1963

TO GOD BE THE GLORY

—W. Howard Doane, 1875

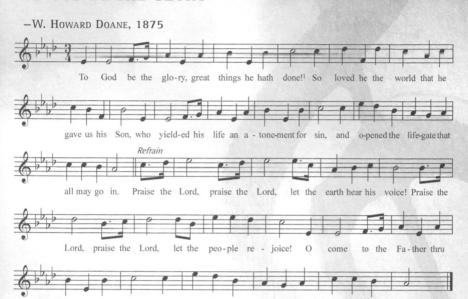

To God be the glo-ry, great things he hath done![1] So loved he the world that he gave us his Son, who yield-ed his life an a - tone-ment for sin, and o-pened the life-gate that all may go in.

Refrain

Praise the Lord, praise the Lord, let the earth hear his voice! Praise the Lord, praise the Lord, let the peo-ple re - joice! O come to the Fa - ther thru Je - sus the Son, and give him the glo - ry, great things he hath done.

2. O perfect redemption, the purchase of blood,[2]
   To every believer the promise of God;[3]
   The vilest offender who truly believes,
   That moment from Jesus a pardon receives.
   Refrain

3. Great things he has taught us, great things he has done,
   And great our rejoicing through Jesus the Son;
   But purer, and higher, and greater will be
   Our wonder, our transport, when Jesus we see.
   Refrain

1. Romans 16:26-27
2. Ephesians 1:6-8
3. 2 Corinthians 1:20-22

—Fanny J. Crosby, 1875

BE THOU MY VISION

—IRISH, 8TH CENTURY

Be thou my vi-sion, O Lord of my heart; naught be all else to me
save that thou art. Thou my best thought, by day or by night,
wak-ing or sleep-ing, thy pres-ence my light.[1]

1. 2 Corinthians 4:6
2. Psalm 115:9
3. Psalm 61:3
4. Revelation 11:15
5. Revelation 22:5

2. Be thou my wisdom, and whou my true Word;
I ever with thee and thou with me, Lord;
Thou my great Father, and I thy true son;
Thou in me dwelling, and I with thee one.

3. Be thou my battle shield, sword for the fight;[2]
Be thou my dignity, thou my delight;
Thou my soul's shelter, thou my high tower.[3]
Raise thou me heavenward, O power of my power.

4. Riches I heed not, nor man's empty praise,
Thou mine inheritance, now and always:
Thou and thou only, first in my heart,
High King of heaven, my treasure thou art.

5. High King of heaven, my victory won,[4]
May I reach heaven's joys, O bright heaven's sun![5]
Heart of my own heart, whatever befall,
Still be my vision, O ruler of all.

—DALLAN FORGAILL, 8TH CENTURY

SEASON AFTER PENTECOST

We find You in joy or in sorrow—still walking alongside, our Helper. We pray, we sing, we dance, we weep. And it's all with You right there alongside us. This is our life, this is our joy, this is our eternal destiny.

In You we live and move and have our being.

LET ME TOUCH LIVES

All through this day, O Lord, by the power of Thy quickening Spirit,
let me touch the lives of others for good, whether through the word
I speak, the prayer I speak, or the life I live.

—Anonymous

MY GOD, I LOVE THEE

My God, I love Thee; not because
I hope for heaven thereby,
Nor yet because who love Thee not
May eternally die.

Thou, O my Jesus, Thou didst me
Upon the cross embrace;
For me didst bear the nails and spear,
And manifold disgrace.

And griefs and torments numberless,
And sweat of agony;
E'en death itself; and all for man
Who was Thine enemy.

Then why, O Beloved Jesus Christ,
Should I not love Thee well?
Not for the hope of winning heaven,
Nor of escaping hell.

Not with the hope of gaining aught,
Nor seeking a reward,
But as Thyself hast loved me,
O everlasting Lord!

E'en so I love Thee, and will love,
And in Thy praise will sing,
Solely because Thou art my God,
And my eternal King.

—Francis Xavier, 1506-1552

WHAT WONDROUS LOVE IS THIS?

—AMERICAN, 19TH CENTURY

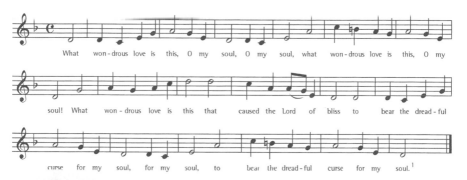

What won-drous love is this, O my soul, O my soul, what won-drous love is this, O my soul! What won-drous love is this that caused the Lord of bliss to bear the dread-ful curse for my soul, for my soul, to bear the dread-ful curse for my soul.[1]

2. When I was sinking down, sinking down, sinking down,
When I was sinking down, sinking down,
When I was sinking down beneath God's righteous frown,
Christ laid aside His crown for my soul, for my soul,
Christ laid aside His crown for my soul.[2]

3. To God and to the Lamb, I will sing, I will sing;[3]
To God and to the Lamb, I will sing.
To God and to the Lamb Who is the great "I Am";
While millions join the theme, I will sing, I will sing;
While millions join the theme, I will sing.

4. And when from death I'm free, I'll sing on, I'll sing on;
And when from death I'm free, I'll sing on.[4]
And when from death I'm free, I'll sing and joyful be;
And through eternity, I'll sing on, I'll sing on;
And through eternity, I'll sing on.

1. Galatians 3:9-14
2. Romans 5:8
3. Revelation 7:10
4. Revelation 21:3-5

—WILLIAM WALKER, 1835

GOODNESS AND MERCY FOLLOW ME

Unnumbered comforts to my soul
Thy tender care bestowed,
Before my infant heart conceived
From Whom those comforts flowed.

When in the slippery paths of youth
With heedless steps I ran,
Thine arm unseen conveyed me safe,
And led me up to man.

Ten thousand precious gifts
My daily thanks employ;
Nor is the last a cheerful heart
That tastes those gifts with joy.

When worn with sickness, oft hast Thou
With health renewed my face;
And, when in sins and sorrows sunk,
Revived my soul with grace.

Through every period of my life
Thy goodness I'll pursue
And after death, in distant worlds,
The glorious theme renew.

—JOSEPH ADDISON, 1672-1719

BECAUSE OF YOUR BLOOD

Thank you, Father, for the blood that covers even me.
I could never fathom it, earn it, ignore it or refuse it.
I simply and humbly accept it.
Because of your blood, I am yours and you are mine.

—JEANNETTE MANCHESTER, 1980-

I LOVE THE LORD GOD

I love the Lord God with all my weakness and inhibition.
I turn to Him in trust as I fall before His feet.
I see in Him the swallow of each tear that casts a shadow.
I bring to Him a heart sobbing in relief.

—ANONYMOUS

THINK ABOUT HIS LOVE

—Walt Harrah, 1987

1. How could I forget His love?
   How could I forget His mercy?
   He satisfies, He satisfies,
   He satisfies my desires.[4]
   Great is the measure of our Father's love.

   Refrain

2. Even when I've strayed away
   His love has sought me out and found me.
   He satisfies, He satisfies,
   He satisfies my desires.
   Great is the measure of our Father's love.

—Walt Harrah, 1987

1. Titus 3:4-5
2. Psalm 103:11
3. 1 John 3:1
4. Psalm 37:4

THE POTTER'S HAND

—Darlene Zschech, 1997

Beau-ti-ful Lord, won-der-ful Sav - ior, I know for sure all of my days are held in Your hand; Craft-ed in - to Your per - fect plan.[1] You gent-ly call me in-to Your pres - ence, guid-ing me by Your Ho-ly Spir - it; Teach me, dear Lord, to live all of my life through Your eyes. I'm cap-tured by Your ho-ly call - ing.[2] Set me a-part, I know You're draw - ing me to Your-self;[3] Lead me, Lord, I pray.

Chorus

Take me, mold me, use me, fill me; I give my life to the Pot - ter's hand.[4] Call me, guide me, lead me, walk be - side me; I give my life to the Pot - ter's hand.

1. Romans 8:28-30
2. 2 Corinthians 4:5
3. Psalm 4:3
4. Isaiah 64:8

—Darlene Zschech, 1997

LORD, I GIVE YOU MY HEART

—Reuben Morgan, 1995

Lord, I give you my heart, I give you my soul, I live for You a-lone. Ev-'ry breath that I take, ev-'ry mo-ment I'm a-wake, Have Your way in me. This is my de - sire, to ho - nor You. Lord, with all my heart, I wor-ship You. All I have with-in me I give You praise All that I a-dore is in You.

—Reuben Morgan, 1995

FIRST SUNDAY OF
THE SEASON AFTER PENTECOST

O God, strength of all that put their trust in you, mercifully accept our prayers; and because through the weakness of our mortal nature, we can do no good thing without you, grant us the help of your grace, that in keeping your commandments we may please you both in will and deed, through Jesus Christ our Lord. Amen.

—THOMAS CRANMER, 1489-1556

THAT WHICH I AM

That which I am and the way I am, with all my gifts of nature and grace, You have given to me, O Lord, and You are all this. I offer it all to You, principally to praise You and to help my fellow Christians and myself.

—ANONYMOUS

OH, THE DEEP, DEEP LOVE OF JESUS

—Thomas J. Williams, 1890

O the deep, deep love of Je - sus, Vast, un - mea - sured, bound - less free,[1]
Roll - ing as a might - y o - cean In its full - ness o - ver me.
Un - der - neath me, all a - round me, Is the cur - rent of Thy love;[2]
Lead - ing on - ward, lead - ing home - ward To my glo - rious rest a - bove.

2. Oh, the deep, deep love of Jesus, spread His praise from shore to shore!
How He loveth, ever loveth, changeth never, nevermore!
How He watches o'er His loved ones, died to call them all His own;
How for them He intercedeth, watcheth o'er them from the throne![3]

3. Oh, the deep, deep love of Jesus, love of every love the best!
'Tis an ocean vast of blessing, 'tis a haven sweet of rest!
Oh, the deep, deep love of Jesus, 'tis a heaven of heavens to me;
And it lifts me up to glory, for it lifts me up to Thee!

1. Romans 8:35
2. Ephesians 3:18-19
3. Psalm 121:4

—Samuel T. Francis, 1875

PASSIONATE OBEDIENCE

I want passionate feelings to characterize my relationship with the Lord Jesus. Of course, I want to be perfectly obedient to the Lord, but I want the obedience to spring out of a passionate love for Him. I want to obey Jesus not simply out of discipline or duty, or because of some reward or fear of punishment. I want to serve Him simply for the joy of being able to please the one I love so much.

—JACK DEERE, n.d.

AWARENESS

To the left. To the right. Behind me. Ahead of me.
I am aware of you. Your presence.
Thank you for walking close by, Lord.
Help me to walk this dusty path of life
and intentionally engage with fellow travelers
who may at this time be yet unaware of you.

—ANONYMOUS

GIVE HIM TIME

We say, then, to anyone who is under trial, give Him time to steep the soul in His eternal truth. Go into the open air, look up into the depths of the sky, or out upon the wideness of the sea, or on the strength of the hills that is His also; or, if bound in the body, go forth in the spirit; spirit is not bound. Give Him time and, as surely as dawn follows night, there will break upon the heart a sense of certainty that cannot be shaken.

—AMY CARMICHAEL, 1867–1951

BE STILL, MY SOUL

—JEAN SIBELIUS, 1899

Be still, my soul: the Lord is on your side. Bear pa-tient-ly the
cross of grief or pain;[1] leave to your God to or-der and pro-vide;
in ev-ery change God faith-ful will re - main. Be still, my soul: your
best, your heaven-ly friend through thorn-y ways leads to a joy-ful end.

2. Be still, my soul: thy God doth undertake
   To guide the future as He has the past.
   Thy hope, thy confidence let nothing shake;
   All now mysterious shall be bright at last.
   Be still, my soul: the waves and winds still know
   His voice Who ruled them while He dwelt below.[2]

3. Be still, my soul: when dearest friends depart,
   And all is darkened in the vale of tears,
   Then shalt thou better know His love, His heart,
   Who comes to soothe thy sorrow and thy fears.
   Be still, my soul: thy Jesus can repay
   From His own fullness all He takes away.[3]

4. Be still, my soul: the hour is hastening on
   When we shall be forever with the Lord.[4]
   When disappointment, grief, and fear are gone,
   Sorrow forgot, love's purest joys restored.
   Be still, my soul: when change and tears are past[5]
   All safe and blessèd we shall meet at last.

5. Be still, my soul: begin the song of praise
   On earth, be leaving to Thy Lord on high;
   Acknowledge Him in all thy words and ways,[6]
   So shall He view thee with a well-pleased eye.
   Be still, my soul: the Sun of life divine
   Through passing clouds shall but more brightly shine.

1. Matthew 10:38
2. Matthew 8:26
3. Matthew 19:29
4. 1 Thessalonians 4:17
5. Revelation 21:4
6. Proverbs 3:6

—KATHARINA A. D. VON SCHLEGEL, 1752

THE NAME

If you want to touch God's heart, use the name he loves to hear.
Call him Father.

—MAX LUCADO, 1955-

STILL

—REUBEN MORGAN, 1999

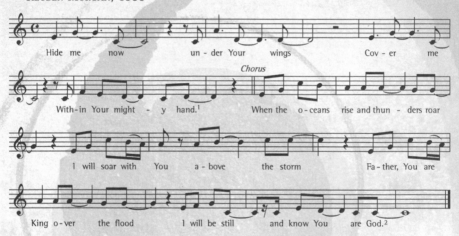

Hide me now un-der Your wings Cov - er me With-in Your might - y hand.[1] When the o-ceans rise and thun - ders roar I will soar with You a - bove the storm Fa - ther, You are King o - ver the flood I will be still and know You are God.[2]

Chorus

2. Find rest, my soul,
   In Christ alone.[3]
   Know His power
   In quietness and trust.

   1. Psalm 17:7-9
   2. Psalm 46:10
   3. Matthew 11:29

—REUBEN MORGAN, 1999

SECOND SUNDAY OF
THE SEASON AFTER PENTECOST

O Lord, who never fails to help and govern whom you bring up in your steadfast fear and love; keep us, we ask you, under the protection of your good providence, and give us perpetual fear and love for your Holy name; through Jesus Christ our Lord. Amen.

—THOMAS CRANMER, 1489-1556

IF GOD WERE SMALL

If God were small enough to be understood, He would not be big enough to be worshiped.

—EVELYN UNDERHILL, 1875-1941

THY WILL BE DONE

Thy will be done. I yield up everything.
"The life is more than meat"—then more than health;
"The body more than raiment"—then more than wealth;
The hairs I made not, thou art numbering.
Thou art my life—I the brook, thou the spring.
Because thine eyes are open, I can see;
Because thou art thyself, 'tis therefore I am me.

—GEORGE MACDONALD, 1824-1905

WHERE THE SPIRIT WORKS

Where the Holy Spirit works, He kindles . . .
sighs,
groans,
supplications,
wrestlings, and
pleadings.

To know Christ, feel His love, taste the efficacy of His atoning blood,
and embrace Him as all our salvation and all our desire.

And though there may, and doubtless will be, much barrenness,
hardness, deadness, and apparent carelessness
often felt; still that heavenly Teacher will
revive His work, though often by
painful methods; nor will He let
the quickened soul rest short
of a personal and experi-
mental enjoyment of
Christ and His glorious
salvation.

—J. C. PHILPOT, 1802-1869

SING PRAISE TO GOD WHO REIGNS ABOVE

—KIRCHENGESANGE, 1556

Sing praise to God who reigns a-bove, The God of all cre - a - tion,[1] The
God of pow'r, the God of love, The God of our sal - va - tion. With heal-ing balm my
soul He fills, And ev-'ry faith-less mur-mur stills: To God all praise and glo - ry!

2. What God's almighty power hath made His gracious mercy keepeth,
   By morning glow or evening shade His watchful eye ne'er sleepeth;
   Within the kingdom of His might, Lo! all is just and all is right:
   To God all praise and glory.

3. The Lord is never far away, but through all grief distressing,[2]
   An ever present help and stay, our peace and joy and blessing.[3]
   As with a mother's tender hand, God gently leads the chosen band:
   To God all praise and glory.

4. Thus, all my toilsome way along, I sing aloud Thy praises,
   That earth may hear the grateful song my voice unwearied raises.
   Be joyful in the Lord, my heart, both soul and body bear your part:
   To God all praise and glory.

5. Let all who name Christ's holy Name give God all praise and glory;
   Let all who own His power proclaim aloud the wondrous story!
   Cast each false idol from its throne, for Christ is Lord, and Christ alone:
   To God all praise and glory.

1. Psalm 97:1
2. Psalm 73:28
3. Psalm 46:1

—JOHANN J. SCHUTZ, 1675

I WORSHIP YOU, ALMIGHTY GOD

—Sondra Corbett, 1983

I wor - ship You, Al - might - y God, there is none like You,[1] I

wor - ship You, O Prince of Peace, that is what I want to do. I

give You praise for You are my right-eous - ness I wor-ship You, Al -

might - y God, there is none like You.

1. Jeremiah 10:7

—Sondra Corbett, 1983

WILD WONDER

What I believe is so magnificent, so glorious, that it is beyond finite comprehension. To believe that the universe was created by a purposeful, benign Creator is one thing. To believe that this Creator took on human vesture, accepted death and mortality, was tempted, betrayed, broken, and all for love of us, defies reason. It is so wild that it terrifies some Christians who try to dogmatize their fear by lashing out at other Christians, because tidy Christianity with all answers given is easier than one which reaches out to the wild wonder of God's love, a love we don't even have to earn.

—MADELEINE L'ENGLE, 1918–

TRUE FAITH

True faith is not a mere passive impression, or an inoperative notion. It is a holy principle wrought in the soul by the Spirit of God, producing gracious habits, holy affections, filial reverence and obedience. True faith is seated in the heart, influencing and purifying the whole inner man. True faith unites the soul to Christ, as the branch to the vine. It draws virtue from him, whereby the believer is rendered fruitful in every good work. The sweet fruits of the Spirit appear and abound in rich luxuriance on these favored branches, to the glory of God.

—THOMAS READE, 1841–1909

211

ABSOLUTE BEAUTY

I believe there is nothing lovelier, deeper, more sympathetic, and more perfect than the Savior; there is in the world only one figure of absolute beauty: Christ.

—Fyodor Dostoevsky, 1821–1881

THIRD SUNDAY OF
THE SEASON AFTER PENTECOST

O Lord, you mercifully hear us; grant that we, to whom you have given a hearty desire to pray, may by your mighty aid be defended and comforted in all dangers and adversities; through Jesus Christ our Lord. Amen.

—Thomas Cranmer, 1489–1556

FIRE OF LOVE

Holy Spirit, fire of love, come rest over each of us; make our tongue ready to confess our sins, that in revealing everything and conceal-ing nothing, we may attain heavenly life to sing eternal praise with the angels. With your help, you who live and reign through all ages. Amen.

—Anthony of Padua, 1195–1231

THE ADORABLE SPIRIT

The adorable Spirit comes in Christ's name. He teaches what Christ taught. He takes of the things of Christ, and reveals them unto us. From the infinite fund of scriptural wisdom and knowledge—He draws and dispenses, according to the diversified necessities of His people. It is scarcely a change of teacher. The Spirit gives the same lessons as Jesus. He repeats and revives them. He brings out afresh in the chambers of memory the truths which had faded. He touches the sluggish heart to awaken it to new impressions of scriptural truth. All this is by a direct influence on the soul by the Spirit—opening the mind and pouring in light.

—JAMES W. ALEXANDER, 1804-1859

YOU CANNOT LIVE WITHOUT THE HOLY SPIRIT

There cannot be one heavenly aspiration, one breathing of love, one upward glance of faith without His gracious influences. Apart from Him, there is no preciousness in the Word, no blessing in ordinances, no permanent, sanctifying results in affliction.

The Holy Spirit directs His people to the waters of comfort, gives new glory to the promises, and invests the Savior's character and work with new loveliness and beauty.

Come, then, with your affliction!
Come with your infirmity!
Come with your need!
Come with your wounded spirit!
Come with your broken heart!

Whatever, then, be your present situation, seek the promised help of the Holy Spirit.

—JOHN MACDUFF, 1818-1895

YOU ARE GOOD

—ISRAEL HOUGHTON, 2001

Lord, You are good and Your mer-cy en-dures - for-ev - er.[1]

Lord, You are good and Your mer-cy en-dures - for-ev - er.

Peo - ple from ev - e - ry na-tion and tongue, from gen - er - a - tion to

gen - er - a-tion[2] We wor - ship You, Hal - le - lu - jah, Hal -

le - lu - jah, We wor - ship You for who You are,

'cause You are good. You are good all the time

all the time You are good.

1. 1 Chronicles 16:34
2. Psalm 105:8

—ISRAEL HOUGHTON, 2001

EVERYDAY

—Joel Houston, 1999

What to say, Lord, it's You who gave me life and I
can't explain just how much You mean to me now
that You have saved me, Lord I give all that I am to You;
that ev-ry day I would be a light that shines Your

Refrain

name Ev-'ry day it's You I live for; Ev-ry-day I'll fol-low af-ter
You Ev-'ry day I'll walk with You, my Lord.

2. Everyday, Lord,
   I'll learn to stand upon Your Word.
   And I pray that
   I may come to know You more,
   That You would guide me
   In every single step I take,
   That everyday I can be Your
   Light unto the world.
       Refrain

—Joel Houston, 1999

216

DAY BY DAY

Day by day, dear Lord, of thee three things I pray:
To see thee more clearly,
Love thee more dearly,
Follow thee more nearly, day by day. Amen.

—RICHARD OF CHICHESTER, 1197–1253

A BRUISED FLOWER

Are you as a broken stem? Does some heavy trial now bow you in the dust? Oh, never, perhaps, were you so truly beautiful; never did your grace send forth such fragrance, or your prayers ascend with so sweet an odor; never did faith, and hope, and love develop their hidden glories so richly, so fully as now!

In the eyes of a wounded, a bruised, and a humbled Christ, you were never more lovely, and never more precious to His heart than now.

—OCTAVIUS WINSLOW, 1808–1878

WHEN MORNING GILDS THE SKIES

—JOSEPH BARNBY, 1868

When morn-ing gilds the skies my heart a-wak-ing cries: May Je - sus Christ be praised!

A - like at work and prayer, to Je-sus I re - pair: May Je - sus Christ be praised!

2. When you begin the day, O never fail to say,
   May Jesus Christ be praised!
   And at your work rejoice, to sing with heart and voice,
   May Jesus Christ be praised!

3. To God, the Word, on high, the host of angels cry,
   May Jesus Christ be praised!
   Let mortals, too, upraise their voice in hymns of praise,
   May Jesus Christ be praised!

4. The night becomes as day when from the heart we say:
   May Jesus Christ be praised!
   The powers of darkness fear when this sweet chant they hear:
   May Jesus Christ be praised!

5. Let all the earth around ring joyous with the sound:
   May Jesus Christ be praised!
   In Heaven's eternal bliss the loveliest strain is this:
   May Jesus Christ be praised!

6. Sing, suns and stars of space, sing, ye that see His face,
   Sing, Jesus Christ be praised!
   God's whole creation o'er, for aye and evermore
   Shall Jesus Christ be praised!

7. Be this, while life is mine, my canticle divine:
   May Jesus Christ be praised!
   Sing this eternal song through all the ages long:
   May Jesus Christ be praised!

—GERMAN, C. 1800

UNFLAWED BEGINNINGS

We may never, this side of death, drive the invader out of our territory, but we must be in the Resistance, not in the Vichy government. And this, so far as I can yet see, must be begun again every day. Our morning prayer should be that in the Imitation: Da hodie perfecte incipere—grant me to make an unflawed beginning today, for I have done nothing yet.

—C. S. LEWIS, 1898-1963

FOURTH SUNDAY OF
THE SEASON AFTER PENTECOST

O God, protector of all that trust in you, without whom nothing is strong, nothing is holy: increase and multiply upon us your mercy; that, you being our ruler and guide, we may surpass through things temporal, and finally lose not things that are eternal: Grant this, O Heavenly Father, for Jesus Christ's sake, our Lord. Amen.

—THOMAS CRANMER, 1489-1556

HOW GREAT ARE YOU, LORD

—Lynn DeShazo, 1999

How great are You, Lord, How great is Your mer - cy,[1]

How great are the things that You have done for me

How great are You, Lord, Your lov-ing kind - ness

Fine

is fill-ing my heart as I sing[2] how great are You, Lord

How great is Your love, It reach - es to the heav - ens,[3]

D.C. al Fine

How great is the heart that sought and res - cued me;

1. Psalm 119:156
2. 2 Chronicles 20:20-22
3. Psalm 36:5

—Lynn DeShazo, 1999

MOST HIGH, GLORIOUS GOD

Most High, glorious God, enlighten the darkness of my heart and give me true faith, certain hope, and perfect charity, sense and knowledge, Lord, that I may carry out Your holy and true command. Amen.

—FRANCIS OF ASSISI, 1182–1226

THE SPIRIT'S PRESENCE

Life, comfort, light, purity, power, peace; and many other precious blessings are inseparable from the Spirit's blessed presence.

—CHARLES SPURGEON, 1834–1892

THE BOOK OF NATURE

The book of nature is an expression of the thoughts of God.

We have God's terrible thoughts in the thunder and lightning; God's loving thoughts in the sunshine and the balmy breeze; God's bounteous, prudent, careful thoughts in the waving harvest and in the ripening meadow.

We have God's brilliant thoughts in the wondrous scenes which are beheld from mountain-top and valley; and we have God's most sweet and pleasant thoughts of beauty in the little flowers that blossom at our feet.

—CHARLES SPURGEON, 1834–1892

ALL CREATURES OF OUR GOD AND KING

—Geistliche Kirchensesänge, 1623

All crea-tures of our God and King, lift up your voice and with us sing,

O praise ye! Al - le - lu - ia! Thou burn-ing sun with gold-en beam,[1] Thou

Refrain

sil-ver moon with sof-ter gleam! O praise ye! O praise ye! Al - le -

lu - ia! Al - le - lu - ia! Al - le lu - ia!

2. Thou rushing wind that art so strong,
Ye clouds that sail in heaven along,
O praise Him! Alleluia!
Thou rising morn, in praise rejoice,
Ye lights of evening, find a voice!
   Refrain

3. Thou flowing water, pure and clear,
Make music for thy Lord to hear,
O praise Him! Alleluia!
Thou fire so masterful and bright,
That givest man both warmth and light.
   Refrain

4. And all ye men of tender heart,
Forgiving others, take your part,[2]
O sing ye! Alleluia!
Ye who long pain and sorrow bear,
Praise God and on Him cast your care![3]
   Refrain

5. Let all things their Creator bless,[4]
And worship Him in humbleness,
O praise Him! Alleluia!
Praise, praise the Father, praise
   the Son,
And praise the Spirit, Three in One!
   Refrain

1. Psalm 19:1-6
2. John 20:22-23
3. 1 Peter 5:7
4. Psalm 150:6

—Francis of Assisi, 1225

SHOUT TO THE LORD

—Darlene Zschech, 1996

1. Jeremiah 10:6
2. Psalm 71:21
3. Psalm 61:3
4. Psalm 67:3-4
5. Psalm 41:12

—Darlene Zschech, 1996

THE SACRED HEART

The sacred heart of Christ is an inexhaustible fountain, and its sole desire is to pour itself out into the hearts of the humble so as to free them and prepare them to lead lives according to his good pleasure.

—SAINT MARGARET MARY ALACOQUE, 1647-1690

A LOVE GIFT

Worship is giving God the best that He has given you. Be careful what you do with the best you have. Whenever you get a blessing from God, give it back to Him as a love gift. Take time to meditate before God and offer the blessing back to Him in a deliberate act of worship.

—OSWALD CHAMBERS, 1874-1917

ARMS OF FAITH

Now, with the arms of my faith, I clasp the promise—and Jesus in the promise! Here will I live, and here will I die, blessing God, who causes me always to triumph in Jesus Christ my Lord!

—JAMES MEIKLE, 1730-1799

WORTHY, YOU ARE WORTHY

Don Moen, 1986

Wor - thy, You are wor - thy,[1] King of Kings, Lord of lords,[2] You are wor - thy.

Wor - thy, You are wor - thy, King of Kings, Lord of lords, I wor-ship You.[3]

2. Holy, You are Holy.[4]
King of kings, Lord of lords,
You are Holy,
Holy, You are Holy.
King of kings, Lord of lords,
I worship You.

3. Jesus, You are Jesus.
King of kings, Lord of lords,
You are Jesus.
Jesus, You are Jesus.
King of kings, Lord of lords,
I worship you.

1. Revelation 4:11
2. Revelation 19:16
3. Psalm 66:4
4. Revelation 4:8

—Don Moen, 1986

FIFTH SUNDAY OF
THE SEASON AFTER PENTECOST

Grant, O Lord, that the course of this world may be so peacefully ordered by your governance, that your Church may joyfully serve you in all godly quietness; through Jesus Christ our Lord. Amen.

—THOMAS CRANMER, 1489-1556

PEACE PRAYER

Lord, make me an instrument of Thy peace; where there is hatred, let me sow love; where there is injury, pardon; where there is doubt, faith; where there is despair, hope; where there is darkness, light; and where there is sadness, joy.

O Divine Master, grant that I may not so much seek to be consoled as to console; to be understood, as to understand; to be loved, as to love; for it is in giving that we receive, it is in pardoning that we are pardoned, and it is in dying that we are born to eternal life.

—FRANCIS OF ASSISI, 1182-1226

SAVIOR, LIKE A SHEPHERD LEAD US

—WILLIAM B. BRADBURY, 1859

2. We are Thine, Thou dost befriend us, be the guardian of our way;
   Keep Thy flock, from sin defend us, seek us when we go astray.[3]
   Blessèd Jesus, blessèd Jesus! Hear, O hear us when we pray.
   Blessèd Jesus, blessèd Jesus! Hear, O hear us when we pray.

3. Thou hast promised to receive us, poor and sinful though we be;
   Thou hast mercy to relieve us, grace to cleanse and power to free.
   Blessèd Jesus, blessèd Jesus! We will early turn to Thee.
   Blessèd Jesus, blessèd Jesus! We will early turn to Thee.

4. Early let us seek Thy favor, early let us do Thy will;
   Blessèd Lord and only Savior, with Thy love our bosoms fill.
   Blessèd Jesus, blessèd Jesus! Thou hast loved us, love us still.
   Blessèd Jesus, blessèd Jesus! Thou hast loved us, love us still.

1. Psalm 23:1-2
2. Hebrews 10:19-22
3. John 10:3

—DOROTHY A. THRUPP, 1836

THE GOOD SHEPHERD

Who is He of whom such gracious words are spoken? He is the good
Shepherd. Why does He carry the lambs in His bosom? Because He
has a tender heart, and any weakness at once melts His heart.

The sighs, the ignorance, the feebleness of the little ones of His flock
draw forth His compassion.

—CHARLES SPURGEON, 1834–1892

O THOU, THE PRIMAL FOUNT

O Thou, the primal fount of life and peace,
 Who shed'st Thy breathing quiet all around,
In me command that pain and conflict cease,
 And turn to music every jarring sound.

—J. STERLING, 1806-1844

THOU HAST MADE US

Thou hast made us for Thyself, O Lord;
and our heart is restless until it rests in Thee.

—AUGUSTINE OF HIPPO, 354-430

COME AS MARY MAGDALENE

When you engage in the duty of prayer, or come to the Lord's Supper, or attend any other duty of divine worship— come to Christ as Mary Magdalene did! Come, and cast yourself at His feet, and kiss them, and pour forth upon Him the sweet perfumed ointment of divine love, out of a pure and broken heart, as she poured the precious perfume out of her pure, broken alabaster jar!

—JONATHAN EDWARDS, 1703–1758

TEARS IN A BOTTLE

Though the Lord is exalted, yet He has regard unto the humble. He has not despised the affliction of His afflicted children, nor hid His face from them. I am poor and needy, yet the Lord thinks upon me. Put my tears into Your bottle.

—NEWMAN HALL, 1816–1902

THE LORD'S MY SHEPHERD

—JESSIE S. IRVINE, 1872

The Lord's my shep-herd, I'll not want. He makes me down to lie in pas-tures green; he lead-eth me the qui-et wa-ters by.[1]

2. My soul he doth restore again;
   And me to walk doth make
   Within the paths of righteousness,
   Even for his own Name's sake.[2]

3. Yea, though I walk in death's dark vale,
   Yet will I fear no ill;
   For thou art with me; and thy rod
   And staff me comfort still.[3]

4. My table thou hast furnishèd
   In presence of my foes;
   My head thou dost with oil anoint,
   And my cup overflows.[4]

5. Goodness and mercy all my life
   Shall surely follow me;
   And in God's house forevermore
   My dwelling place shall be.[5]

1. Psalm 23:1-2
2. Psalm 23:3
3. Psalm 23:4
4. Psalm 23:5
5. Psalm 23:6

—SCOTTISH PSALTER, 1650

SIXTH SUNDAY OF
THE SEASON AFTER PENTECOST

*O God, who has prepared for those that love you such good things
as pass man's understanding; pour into our hearts love toward you,
that we, loving you above all things, may obtain your promises,
which exceed all that we can desire, through Jesus Christ our Lord.
Amen.*

—THOMAS CRANMER, 1489-1556

THE NATURE OF GOODNESS

That is why the Christian is in a different position from other people
who are trying to be good. They hope, by being good, to please God
if there is one; or—if they think there is not—at least they hope to
deserve approval from good men. But the Christian thinks any good
he does comes from the Christ-life inside him. He does not think God
will love us because we are good, but that God will make us good
because He loves us; just as the roof of a greenhouse does not attract
the sun because it is bright, but becomes bright because the sun
shines on it.

—C. S. LEWIS, 1898-1963

GOD IS GOOD

God is good. This is the prime statement about God's character. From it flow all others. To be good means to be good. God is goodness. That is, what he is is good. There is no sense in which goodness surpasses God or God surpasses goodness. As being is the essence of his nature, goodness is the essence of his character.

—James W. Sire, 1933-

GRATEFUL FOR GOD'S GOODNESS

God's goodness hath been great to thee;
Let never day or night unhallowed pass,
But still remember what the Lord hath done.

—William Shakespeare, 1564-1616

THE NATURE OF GOODNESS

Goodness is love in action, love with its hand to the plow, love with the burden on its back, love following His footsteps who went about continually doing good.

—James Hamilton, 1974-

MIGHTY IS OUR GOD

—Eugene Greco, Gerrit Gustafson, and Don Moen, 1987

Might-y is our God   Might-y is our King[1]

Might-y is our Lord.   Ru-ler of ev-ry-thing

Glo-ry to our God   Glo-ry to our King

Glo-ry to our Lord   Ru-ler of ev-ry-thing   His name is

high-er   high-er than an-y oth-er name[2]   His pow'r is

great-er for He has cre-a-ted ev-'ry thing

1. Psalm 89:8
2. Psalm 83:18

—Eugene Greco, Gerrit Gustafson, and Don Moen, 1987

BLESSED BE THE LORD GOD ALMIGHTY

—Bob Fitts, 1984

2. O God, most Holy, we adore You,
   We lay our all before Your throne.
   May the fragrance of Your presence be about us
   As we purpose to worship You alone!

   Refrain

1. Psalm 8:1
2. Psalm 72:18
3. Revelation 4:8

—Bob Fitts, 1984

236

HE IS THE RULER

Our God is not a spectator or even a competitor in this world. He is the Ruler of it. Salvation is knowing him, the only true and living God as he is revealed in the Lord Jesus Christ his Son, the God-man, our Savior. He who is our God is the only God you can trust.

—Don Fortner, 1950-

SEVENTH SUNDAY OF
THE SEASON AFTER PENTECOST

Lord of all power and might, author and giver of all good things; graft into our hearts the love of your name, increase in us true religion, nourish us with all goodness, and of your great mercy keep us; through Jesus Christ our Lord. Amen.

—Thomas Cranmer, 1489-1556

ETERNAL LIFE

Eternal life was the life which Jesus Christ exhibited on the human plane, and it is the same life, not a copy of it, which is manifested in our mortal flesh when we are born of God. Eternal life is not a gift from God, eternal life is the gift *of God*. The energy and power which was manifested in Jesus will be manifested in us by the sheer sovereign grace of God when once we have made the moral decision about sin.

—Oswald Chambers, 1874-1917

A FREE ACT OF MERCY

Just as God did not have to create the world in order to make up for some deficiency in the Godhead, even so God is in no way obligated to save people who rebel against him. Salvation, like creation, is a free act of God's mercy.

—TED M. DORMAN, n.d.

GOD SINGS!

There is an unrivaled picture in the Word where the Lord is even represented as "singing with joy over His people." Who could have conceived of the Eternal One as bursting forth into a song? Yet it is written, "He will rejoice over you with joy, he will rest in his love, he will rejoice over you with singing."

As He looked upon the newly created world, He spoke and said, "It is very good," but He did not sing. And as He views the works of providence, I do not read that He sings. But when He gazes on His people, the purchase of Jesus' blood, His own chosen ones, the great heart of the Infinite restrains itself no longer, but, wonder of wonders and miracle of miracles, God, the Eternal One, sings out of the joy of His soul!

—CHARLES SPURGEON, 1834–1892

TRADING MY SORROWS

—D<small>ARRELL</small> E<small>VANS</small>, 1998

I'm trad-ing my sor-rows, I'm trad-ing my shame; [1]
I'm lay-ing them down for the joy of the Lord. I'm trad-ing my
sick-ness, I'm trad-ing my pain; I'm lay-ing it down for the joy of the
Lord. We say yes, Lord, yes, Lord, yes, yes, Lord, yes, Lord, yes, Lord, yes, yes, Lord
yes, Lord, yes, Lord, yes, yes, Lord, A-men. I am pressed but not crushed per-se-
cut-ed, not a-ban-doned; struck down but not de-stroyed. I am blessed
be-yond the curse, for His prom-ise will en-dure, that his joy is gon-na be my strength. [2]
Though the sor-row may last for the night, His joy comes with the morn-ing [3]

1. Isaiah 35:10
2. Nehemiah 8:10
3. Psalm 30:5

—D<small>ARRELL</small> E<small>VANS</small>, 1998

MERCY

With gentle, loving touch, He heals the broken in heart and binds up their wounds. He is as gracious in the manner of His mercy as in the matter of it.

—CHARLES SPURGEON, 1834–1892

GIVE MY HEART WINGS

Provide Thou for my heart, O Lord. It is the only unwinged bird in all creation. Give it wings! O Lord, give it wings! Earth has failed to give it wings; its very power of loving has often drawn it into the mire. Be Thou the strength of my heart. Be Thou its fortress in temptation, its shield in remorse, its cover in the storm, its star in the night, its voice in the solitude. Guide it in its gloom; help it in its heat; direct it in its doubt; calm it in its conflict; fan it in its faintness; prompt it in its perplexity; lead it through its labyrinth; raise it from its ruins.

—MRS. CHARLES E. COWMAN, 1870-1960

ALL IS GRACE

Even if I had performed all the deeds of Saint Paul, I would consider myself an unprofitable servant. I would notice that my hands are empty. But that is precisely the cause of my joy: since I have nothing, I shall expect everything from the good God.

—SAINT THERESE OF LISIEUX, 1873-1897

WE ALL BOW DOWN

—Lenny LeBlanc, 2002

Princ - es and pau - pers, sons and daugh - ters
kneel at the throne of grace Los - ers and win - ners,
saints and sin - ners one day will see His face.

Refrain

And we all bow down. Kings will sur - ren - der their crowns
and wor - ship Je - sus, for He is the love, un -
fail - ing love He is the love of God.

2. Summer and winter
The mountains and rivers
Whisper our Savior's name.
Awesome and holy,
A friend to the lonely,
Forever His love will reign.

Refrain

He's the light of the world
And Lord of the cross.

Refrain

—Lenny LeBlanc, 2002

241

EIGHTH SUNDAY OF THE SEASON AFTER PENTECOST

O God, whose never-failing providence orders all things both in heaven and earth, we humbly implore you to put away from us all hurtful things, and to give us those things which will be profitable for us, through Jesus Christ our Lord. Amen.

—THOMAS CRANMER, 1489-1556

THE POWER OF THE PASSION

Christ's death swallowed up death, and the very centurion said, "Truly this is the Son of God." He is the amazing King. Other kings are strong in life: He in death.... When he was dead the centurion trembled and commenced to be a Christian....The disciples fled, but the centurion began to confess Christ without fear of all the high priests or of what Pilate and the council might say. Who then was master here? Was it not the death of Christ that gave the heathen centurion a new spirit? This is the power of the Passion—that it makes men bold to confess Christ.

—MARTIN LUTHER, 1483-1546

DIFFERENT CHARACTER, SAME GRACE

We must never forget that there are varieties in character, and that
the grace of God does not cast all believers into one and the same
mold. The flowers in a garden may differ widely, and yet the gardener
feels interest in all. The children of a family may be curiously unlike
one another, and yet the parents care for all. It is just so with the
Church of Christ.

—J. C. Ryle, 1816-1900

ROCK IN A WEARY LAND

Oh, Jesus is a rock in a weary land,
A weary land, a weary land,
Oh, Jesus is a rock in a weary land,
A shelter in the time of storm.

—African-American Spiritual

REFUGE FOR THE FAITHFUL

Through Thy captivity, Son of God,
Freedom to us has come,
Thy prison is the throne of grace,
The refuge for all the faithful,
For if Thou hadst not been enslaved
Our slavery would last forever.

—J. S. Bach, 1685-1750

243

I NEED THEE EVERY HOUR

—Robert Lowry, 1872

I need thee ev-ery hour, most gra - cious Lord; no ten - der voice like

Refrain

thine can peace af - ford. I need thee, O I need thee; ev - ery hour I

need thee; O bless me now, my Sav - ior, I come to thee.[1]

2. I need thee every hour, stay thou nearby;
   Temptations lose their power when thou art nigh.
   > *Refrain*

3. I need thee every hour, in joy or pain;
   Come quickly and abide, or life is in vain.
   > *Refrain*

4. I need thee every hour; teach me thy will;
   And thy rich promises in me fulfill.
   > *Refrain*

5. I need thee every hour, most Holy One;
   Oh, make me thine indeed, thou blessèd Son!
   > *Refrain*

1. Psalm 86:1

—Annie S. Hawks, 1872

RICH IN GRACE

How blessed is the thought that God is rich in grace! His throne is a throne of grace. His scepter is a scepter of grace. His covenant is a covenant of grace. His thoughts are thoughts of grace. His ways are ways of grace. His Word is the word of grace. His treasure-house is stored with grace.

Oh, the riches of the grace of our God! While we have breath let us extol and magnify it.

—HENRY LAW, 1797-1884

GOD'S PERSPECTIVE

If you look at the underside of a tapestry, you may see a lot of loose ends or rough spots. That's the way life sometimes looks from our viewpoint. But if we look at the other side, we'll see a beautifully woven work. If we look only at the ugly things coming our way, we may doubt God's blessings. But if we view them from God's perspective, we'll know that God is still in charge and that He can use everything in life to bless us.

—MARIE SHROPSHIRE, 1921-

NINTH SUNDAY OF THE SEASON AFTER PENTECOST

Grant to us, Lord, the spirit to think and do always the things that are right; that we who cannot do anything that is good without you, may by you be enabled to live according to your will, through Jesus Christ our Lord. Amen.

—THOMAS CRANMER, 1489-1556

RISE UP AND PRAISE HIM

—Paul Baloche and Gary Sadler, 1996

Let the har-vest re-joice. let the earth be glad [1]

Let the peo-ple of God sing His praise all o-ver the land

Ev-ry one in the val - ley come and lift your voice [2]

All those on the moun - tain-top be glad and shout for joy [3]

Refrain

Rise up and praise Him He de-serves our love

rise up and praise Him wor-ship the Ho - ly One with all your heart

with all your soul with all your might rise up and praise Him.

1. 1 Chronicles 16:31
2. Isaiah 40:4-5
3. Isaiah 42:11

—Paul Baloche and Gary Sadler, 1996

OPEN THE EYES OF MY HEART

—Paul Baloche, 1997

O-pen the eyes of my heart, Lord,[1] o-pen the eyes of my heart I want to see You.[2] I want to see You. To see You high and lift - ed up [3] Shin-ing in the light of Your glo - ry [4] Pour out Your pow-er and love as we sing, "Ho-ly, Ho - ly, Ho - ly."

1. Psalm 27:8
2. Ephesians 1:18-21
3. Isaiah 52:13
4. 2 Corinthians 4:6

—Paul Baloche, 1997

GLORIFY HIM

Glorify Him in life. In waking and sleeping, glorify Him. In labors and leisure, in joy, in sorrow, in suffering and healing, glorify Him. Shine with excellence in all things, and in all things you will glorify Him.

—JOHN RANDALL DENNIS, 1957–

CREATE IN ME

Create in me that warmth of mercy that shall enable others to find Thy strength for their weakness, Thy peace for their strife, Thy joy for their sorrow, Thy love for their hatred, Thy compassion for their weakness. In Thine own strong name, I pray. Amen.

—PETER MARSHALL, 1902–1949

GOD BE IN MY HEAD

God be in my head, and in my understanding;
God be in mine eyes, and in my looking;
God be in my mouth, and in my speaking;
God be in my heart, and in my thinking;
God be at mine end, and at my departing.

—SARUM PRIMER, 1538

MY FATHER'S WAYS

"I don't think the way you think.
The way you work isn't the way I work."
God's decree.
"For as the sky soars high above the earth,
so the way I work surpasses the way you work,
and the way I think is beyond the way you think.
Just as rain and snow descend from the skies
and don't go back until they've watered the earth,
Doing their work of making things grow and blossom,
producing seed for farmers and food for the hungry,
So will the words that come out of my mouth
not come back empty-handed.
They'll do the work I sent them to do,
they'll complete the assignment I gave them."

—EUGENE PETERSON, 1932–
(FROM ISAIAH 55:8-11 *THE MESSAGE*)

THIS IS MY FATHER'S WORLD

—FRANKLIN L. SHEPPARD, 1915

This is my Fath-er's world, and to my lis-tening ears[1] all na-ture sings, and round me rings the mu-sic of the spheres.

Refrain

This is my Fath-er's world: I rest me in the thought of rocks and trees, of skies and seas; his hand the won-ders wrought.

2. This is my Father's world, the birds their carols raise,
   The morning light, the lily white, declare their Maker's praise.[2]
   This is my Father's world: he shines in all that's fair;
   In the rustling grass I hear him pass;
   He speaks to me everywhere.

3. This is my Father's world. O let me ne'er forget
   That though the wrong seems oft so strong, God is the ruler yet.
   This is my Father's world, the battle is not done:
   Jesus Who died shall be satisfied,
   And earth and Heav'n be one.

4. This is my Father's world, should my heart be ever sad?
   The Lord is King—let the heavens ring. God reigns—let the earth be glad.
   This is my Father's world. Now closer to Heaven bound,
   For dear to God is the earth Christ trod.
   No place but is holy ground.

1. Psalm 24:1
2. Psalm 145:10

—FRANKLIN L. SHEPPARD, 1915

HEAV'N

—African-American Spiritual

I got a robe, you got a robe All of God's Chil-dren got a robe;

When I get to heav-en goin' to put on my robe Goin' to shout all o - ver God's

Heav'-n. Heav'-n, Heav'-n Ev-'ry bod-y talk-in' 'bout heav'n ain't go-in' there

Heav'-n, Heav'-n, Goin' to shout all o - ver God's heav'-n.

2. I've got a crown, you've got a crown,
   All of God's children got a crown.
   When I get to Heaven goin' to put on my crown,
   Goin' to shout all over God's Heav'n.
   Refrain

3. I've got shoes, you've got shoes,
   All of God's children got shoes.
   When I get to Heaven goin' to put on my shoes,
   Goin' to walk all over God's Heav'n.
   Refrain

4. I've got a song, you've got a song,
   All of God's children got a song.
   When I get to Heaven goin' to sing a new song,
   Goin' to sing all over God's Heav'n.
   Refrain

—African-American Spiritual

252

MY FATHER'S WILL

You can calm the troubled mind,
You its dread can still;
Teach me to be all resigned
To my Father's will.

—CHRISTIAN RUDOLPH HEINRICH PUCHTA, 1808–1858

PILGRIMS AND STRANGERS

Our life on earth is but a vapor! We are but pilgrims and strangers on
this earthly ball, mere sojourners, without fixed or settled habitation,
and passing through this world as not our home or resting-place.

—J. C. PHILPOT, 1802–1869

TENTH SUNDAY OF
THE SEASON AFTER PENTECOST

Let your merciful ears, O Lord, be open to the prayers
of your humble servants; and, that they may obtain
their petitions, have them ask only things that
will please you, through Jesus Christ our Lord.
Amen.

—THOMAS CRANMER, 1489-1556

FIRST THINGS FIRST

Our wealth and abundance of human
resources have positioned us to accept a
paradigm that provision precedes vision.
This has been the foundation of building
no-risk faith. This is a tragedy when a part
of the adventure is the discovery that
vision always precedes provision.

—ERWIN RAPHAEL MCMANUS, 1958-

GOD CAN TURN IT AROUND

When we find ourselves in the midst of
cruel sufferings—be they physical afflictions
or adverse circumstances—most of us are
tempted to give up too soon. Rather than
persevere we are ready to throw in the towel,
to put a period where God has only placed a
comma. Don't! At least not yet. No matter how
tough your situation is, God can turn it around.

—RICHARD EXLEY, n.d.

TRUE CONFESSIONS

*"Who do I have in heaven but You? Beside You, I desire nothing on earth.
My flesh may fail me, my heart may fail me—but You are the strength
of my heart."*

I have true confessions to make:

First, I confess that You are near me in my most vulnerable moments.
   When everyone else fails me, even when I fail myself, You do not desert me.
   You are near.
And I confess that whenever You're near, Your nearness is my good.
   Every time. All the time.
So let me draw near to You with a sincere heart, confident in faith, clean.
   Knowing within Your nearness I will find refuge.
   I will receive mercy, kindness, and strength there.

—JOHN RANDALL DENNIS, 1957-

DEVOTIONAL MUSIC

Where there is devotional music, God is always at hand with His
gracious presence.

—J. S. BACH, 1685-1750

EVERY BITTER CUP

If God is willing to help us, who can stay His hand? Every valley shall be exalted, and every mountain and hill be made low. Fountains shall spring up in the wilderness, and a path be opened through the great waters. In His hands are the hearts of all men. He can thwart the malice of foes, or make our enemies to be at peace with us. He who rescued Israel from Egypt, and Jerusalem from Sennacherib, and Daniel from the lions, is still as able to remove from His children every bitter cup—or give them grace to drink it.

—NEWMAN HALL, 1816–1902

WHERE CHISEL MEETS STONE

We are like blocks of stone out of which the sculptor carves the forms of men. The blows of His chisel, which hurt so much, are what make us perfect.

—C. S. LEWIS, 1898–1963

ELEVENTH SUNDAY OF THE SEASON AFTER PENTECOST

O God, who declares your almighty power wonderfully in showing mercy and pity, mercifully grant us such a measure of your grace, that we, running the way of your commandments, may obtain your gracious promises and be made partakers of your heavenly treasure, through Jesus Christ our Lord. Amen.

—THOMAS CRANMER, 1489-1556

THE GOD WHO COMES

God presents himself to us little by little. The whole story of salvation is the story of God who comes.

—CARLO CARRETTO, 1910-1988

LAY HOLD OF CHRIST

May I lay hold of Jesus Christ, and never let him go, until he bless me. Shine into my heart with the bright beam of your heavenly grace. Shed abroad your love in my soul. Give me the witness of the Holy Spirit. Grant that I may taste your goodness here, in the sweet refreshing streams of Gospel joy, until, borne with gladsome wing to the fountain-head in glory, my soul shall be lost in wonder, love, and praise.

—THOMAS READE, 1841-1909

QUESTIONS

There may be another question that needs to be asked beyond "What is God doing?" and that is this: "What is God dreaming?" Is there something that God wants initiated and He's waiting for someone to volunteer?

—Erwin Raphael McManus, 1958–

THE RESOURCES OF CHRIST

Whatever may be the foe with whom you wage this holy war, whatever the obstacle to your advance in the divine life; faith, looking to the blood of Jesus, wielding the cross of Christ, drawing its supplies from the resources of Christ, will enroll you among those who overcome by the blood of the Lamb!

—Octavius Winslow, 1808–1878

A MIGHTY FORTRESS

—Martin Luther, 1529

A might-y for-tress is our God, a bul-wark nev-er fail - ing;[1] our help-er he a-mid the flood of mor-tal ills pre - vail - ing. For still our an-cient foe doth seek to work us woe; his craft and power are great, and armed with cru-el hate, on earth is not his e - qual.

2. Did we in our own strength confide, our striving would be losing;[2]
Were not the right Man on our side, the Man of God's own choosing:
Dost ask who that may be? Christ Jesus, it is he;
Lord Sabaoth, his name, from age to age the same,
And he must win the battle.[3]

3. And though this world, with devils filled, should threaten to undo us,[4]
We will not fear, for God hath willed his truth to triumph through us:
The Prince of Darkness grim, we tremble not for him;
His rage we can endure, for lo, his doom is sure,
One little word shall fell him.

4. That word above all earthly powers, no thanks to them, abideth;
The Spirit and the gifts are ours through him who with us sideth:
Let goods and kindred go, this mortal life also;
The body they may kill: God's truth abideth still,
His kingdom is forever.[5]

1. Psalm 91:2
2. Ephesians 1:18-20
3. Romans 7:22-23
4. Ephesians 6:12
5. Revelation 11:15

—Martin Luther, 1529

FASTING

Do you fast? Give me proof of it by your works. If you see a poor man, take pity on him. If you see a friend being honored, do not envy him. Do not let only your mouth fast, but also the eye and the ear and the feet and the hands and all the members of our bodies. Let the hands fast, by being free of avarice. Let the feet fast, by ceasing to run after sin. Let the eyes fast, by disciplining them not to glare at that which is sinful. Let the ears fast, by not listening to evil talk and gossip. Let the mouth fast from foul words and unjust criticism. For what good is it if we abstain from birds and fishes, but bite and devour our brothers?

—JOHN CHRYSOSTOM, C. 347–407

OVERCOMING SUFFERING

Although the world is full of suffering, it is also full of the overcoming of it.

—HELEN KELLER, 1880–1968

TWELFTH SUNDAY OF
THE SEASON AFTER PENTECOST

Almighty and everlasting God, who is always more ready to hear than we are to pray, who is able to give more than we desire or deserve, pour down upon us the abundance of your mercy, forgiving us for those things that our conscience is afraid of, and giving us those good things which we are not worthy to ask for, but through the merits and meditation of Jesus Christ your Son, our Lord. Amen.

—THOMAS CRANMER, 1489-1556

ON FORGIVENESS

It is perhaps not so hard to forgive a single great injury. But to forgive the incessant provocations of daily life...how can we do it? Only, I think, by remembering where we stand, by meaning our words when we say in our prayers each night, "Forgive us our trespasses as we forgive those who trespass against us." We are offered forgiveness on no other terms. To refuse it is to refuse God's mercy for ourselves. There is not a hint of exceptions, and God means what He says.

—C. S. LEWIS, 1898-1963

WORSHIPING THE DEEPEST WAY

When you feel abandoned by God yet continue to trust him, you worship in the deepest way.

—RICK WARREN, 1954-

A TRUST IN HIM

By the grace of God, I resolved to seek it [faith] unto the end, (1) by absolutely renouncing all dependence, in whole or in part, upon my own works or righteousness; on which I have really grounded my hope of salvation, though I knew it not, from my youth up; (2) by adding to the constant use of the other means of grace, continual prayer for this very real thing, justifying, saving faith, a full reliance on the blood of Christ shed for me; a trust in Him, as my Christ, as my sole justification, sanctification, and redemption.

—JOHN WESLEY, 1703-1791

I GIVE YOU MY HEART

—Reuben Morgan, 1995

Chorus

Lord, I give you my heart, I give you my soul, I live
for You a-lone. Ev-'ry breath that I take, ev-'ry mo-ment I'm a-wake,
Have Your way in me. This is my de-sire,
to ho-nor You. Lord, with all my heart,
I wor-ship You. All I have with-in me I
give You praise All that I a-dore is in You.

—Reuben Morgan, 1995

TRUE PRAYER

Prayer is a sincere, sensible, affectionate pouring out of the heart and soul to God, through Christ, with the strength and assistance of the Holy Spirit, for such things as God has promised, or according to the Word, for the good of the church, with submission, in faith, to the will of God.

—JOHN BUNYAN, 1628-1688

LET ME HEAR YOUR VOICE

Prayer is the blessed means which God has appointed to bring every grace from Christ to the believer. The believer is to let his requests be made known unto God, and for his encouragement God says that the prayer of the upright is His delight. Yes, He says that He loves to hear it. "Let Me hear your voice, let Me see your face! For your voice is pleasant, and you are lovely!"

—WILLIAM HUNTINGTON, 1745-1813

THE BEST PRAYERS

The best prayers often have more groans than words.

—JOHN BUNYAN, 1628-1688

THIRTEENTH SUNDAY OF
TIIE SEASON AFTER PENTECOST

Almighty and merciful God, of whose only gift it comes that your faithful people do for you true and laudable service, grant that we may so faithfully serve you in this life, that we fail not finally to attain your heavenly promises, through the merits of Jesus Christ our Lord. Amen.

—THOMAS CRANMER, 1489-1556

WHERE GOD CLARIFIES

Do what you know you should do, and you will know what to do. God clarifies in the midst of obedience, not beforehand.

—ERWIN RAPHAEL MCMANUS, 1958-

RECKLESS LOVE

Anyone who holds on to life just as it is destroys that life. But if you let it go, reckless in your love, you'll have it forever, real and eternal.

—EUGENE PETERSON, 1932-
(FROM JOHN 12:25 *THE MESSAGE*)

THE GREATEST PRIVILEGE

Avail yourself of the greatest privilege this side of heaven. Jesus Christ died to make this communion and communication with the Father possible.

—BILLY GRAHAM, 1918–

PRAYER FOR THE SEVEN GIFTS OF THE HOLY SPIRIT

We beg the all-merciful Father through thee, his only begotten Son made man for our sake, crucified and glorified for us, to send upon us from his treasure-house the Spirit of sevenfold grace, who rested upon thee in all his fullness:

the spirit of wisdom, enabling us to relish the fruit of the tree
*   of life, which is indeed thyself;*
the gift of understanding: to enlighten our perceptions;
the gift of prudence, enabling us to follow in thy footsteps;
the gift of strength: to withstand our adversary's onslaught;
the gift of knowledge: to distinguish good from evil
*   by the light of thy holy teaching;*
the gift of piety: to clothe ourselves with charity and mercy;
the gift of fear: to withdraw from all ill-doing and live
*   quietly in awe of thy eternal majesty.*

These are the things for which we petition. Grant them for the honor of thy holy name, to which, with the Father and the Holy Ghost, be all honor and glory, thanksgiving, renown, and lordship for ever and ever. Amen.

—SAINT BONAVENTURE, 1217–1274

COME INTO HIS PRESENCE

—U<small>NKNOWN</small>

Come into His pre-sence sing-ing Al - le - lu-ia   Al - le-lu-ia   Al - le-lu- ia.

2. Glory to God, singing Alleluia! Alleluia! Alleluia!
   Glory to God, singing Alleluia! Alleluia! Alleluia!

3. Praise the Lord together, singing Jesus is Lord! Jesus is Lord! Jesus is Lord!
   Praise the Lord together, singing Jesus is Lord! Jesus is Lord! Jesus is Lord!

4. Praise to His name, singing Glory to God! Glory to God! Glory to God!
   Praise to His name, singing Glory to God! Glory to God! Glory to God!

—U<small>NKNOWN</small>

EMBRACE OF LOVE

He whom neither humans nor angels can grasp by knowledge can be embraced by love.

—A<small>NONYMOUS</small>, 14<small>TH CENTURY</small>

YOUR LOVE IS EXTRAVAGANT

—Darrell Evans, 1998

Your love is ex-trav-a-gant. Your friend-ship Ooo in-ti-mate. I find I'm mov-ing to the rhy-thms of Your grace; Your fra-grance is in-tox-i-cat-ing in our se-cret place, Your love is ex-tra-va-gant. Spread wide in the arms of Christ is the love that cov-ers sin; no great-er love have I ev-er known You con-sid-er me a friend, cap-ture my heart a-gain.

—Darrell Evans, 1998

FOURTEENTH SUNDAY OF THE SEASON AFTER PENTECOST

Almighty and everlasting God, give us the increase of faith, hope, love; and that we may obtain that which you promise, make us to love that which you command through Jesus Christ our Lord. Amen.

—THOMAS CRANMER, 1489–1556

CRITICAL FAITH

If our faith is going to be criticized, let it be for the right reasons. Not because we are too emotional, but because we are not emotional enough; not because our passions are so powerful, but because they are so puny; not because we are too affectionate, but because we lack a deep uncompromising affection for Jesus Christ.

BRENNAN MANNING, 1939–

GREAT IS THY FAITHFULNESS

—W. M. Runyan, 1923

Great is Thy faith-ful-ness, O God my Fa-ther; there is no shad-ow of turn-ing with Thee;

Thou chang-est not, Thy com - pas-sions they fail not; as Thou hast been, Thou for - ev-er wilt be.

Refrain

Great is Thy faith-ful-ness! Great is Thy faith-ful-ness! Morn-ing by morn-ing new mer-cies I see;

all I have need-ed Thy hand hath pro - vid-ed; great is Thy faith - ful - ness, Lord, un-to me!

2. Summer and winter and springtime and harvest,
   Sun, moon, and stars in their courses above
   Join with all nature in manifold witness
   To Thy great faithfulness, mercy, and love.

   Refrain

3. Pardon for sin and a peace that endureth,
   Thine own dear presence to cheer and to guide;
   Strength for today and bright hope for tomorrow,
   Blessings all mine, with ten thousand beside!

   Refrain

—Thomas Chisholm, 1923

IS CHRIST REALLY IN MY LIFE?

If I have no desire to serve others, I should question whether Christ is really in my life.

—RICK WARREN, 1954-

WE PRAISE THEE, O GOD

We praise Thee, O God; we acknowledge Thee to be the Lord.
All the earth doth worship Thee, the Father everlasting.

To Thee all angels cry aloud, the heavens and all the powers therein;
To Thee cherubim and seraphim continually do cry.

Holy, holy, holy, Lord God of Sabaoth!
Heaven and earth are full of the majesty of Thy glory.

The glorious company of the apostles praise Thee;
The goodly fellowship of the prophets praise Thee;

The noble army of martyrs praise Thee;
the holy Church throughout all the world doth acknowledge Thee:

The Father of an infinite majesty; Thine adorable true and only Son,
also the Holy Ghost, the comforter.

—Te Deum Laudamus

PERSEVERANT WORSHIP

Perseverant worship honors God and gives us hope.
God finds humble worship irresistible

—JOHN RANDALL DENNIS, 1957–

PRAISE TO THE LORD, THE ALMIGHTY

—GERMAN, 1665

Praise to the Lord, the Al - might-y, the King of cre - a - tion! O my soul, praise him, for he is thy health and sal - va - tion! All ye who hear, now to his tem-ple draw near; join me in glad ad - o - ra - tion!

2. Praise to the Lord, Who o'er all things so wondrously reigneth,[1]
   Shelters thee under his wings, yea, so gently sustaineth![2]
   Hast thou not seen how thy desires e'er have been
   Granted in what he ordaineth?

3. Praise to the Lord, Who hath fearfully, wondrously, made thee;
   Health hath vouchsafed and, when heedlessly falling, hath stayed thee.
   What need or grief ever hath failed of relief?
   Wings of his mercy did shade thee.

4. Praise to the Lord, Who doth prosper thy work and defend thee;
   Surely his goodness and mercy here daily attend thee.
   Ponder anew what the Almighty can do,
   If with his love he befriend thee.

5. Praise to the Lord, O let all that is in me adore him!
   All that hath life and breath, come now with praises before him.[3]
   Let the Amen sound from his people again,
   Gladly for aye we adore him.

1. Daniel 4:17
2. Matthew 23:37
3. Psalm 100:2

—JOACHIM NEANDER, 1680

274

FIFTEENTH SUNDAY OF THE SEASON AFTER PENTECOST

Keep, O Lord, your church with your perpetual mercy: and, because the frailty of man without you cannot help but fall, keep us ever by your help from all things hurtful and lead us to all things profitable for our salvation, through Jesus Christ our Lord. Amen.

—THOMAS CRANMER, 1489-1556

THE CHURCH WILL OUTLIVE THE UNIVERSE

The Church will outlive the universe and so will your role in it.

—RICK WARREN, 1954-

WE ADORE

We adore You, O Lord Jesus Christ,
in this Church and all the Churches of the world,
and we bless You, because
by Your holy Cross You have redeemed the world.

—SAINT FRANCIS OF ASSISI, 1182-1227

BLEST BE THE TIE THAT BINDS

—Hans G. Nägeli; arr. Lowell Mason, 1845

Blest be the tie that binds our hearts in Chris - tian love;[1] the
fel - low - ship of kin - dred minds is like to that a - bove.

2. Before our Father's throne
   We pour our ardent prayers;
   Our fears, our hopes, our aims are one,[2]
   Our comforts and our cares.

3. We share each other's woes,
   Our mutual burdens bear;[3]
   And often for each other flows
   The sympathizing tear.

4. When we asunder part,
   It gives us inward pain;[4]
   But we shall still be joined in heart,
   And hope to meet again.

5. This glorious hope revives[5]
   Our courage by the way;
   While each in expectation lives,
   And longs to see the day.

1. 2 Peter 1:7
2. 1 John 1:6-8
3. Romans 12:10-11
4. Acts 21:12-14
5. Romans 12:11-13

—John Fawcett, 1782

THE LOVE OF GOD

The love of God is greater far than tongue or pen can ever tell;
It goes beyond the highest star, and reaches to the lowest hell;
The guilty pair, bowed down with care, God gave His Son to win;
His erring child He reconciled, and pardoned from his sin.

O love of God, how rich and pure! How measureless and strong!
It shall forevermore endure, the saints' and angels' song.

When years of time shall pass away, and earthly thrones and
    kingdoms fall,
When men, who here refuse to pray, on rocks and hills and
    mountains call,
God's love so sure, shall still endure, all measureless and strong;
Redeeming grace to Adam's race—the saints' and angels' song.

Could we with ink the ocean fill and were the skies of parchment
    made,
Were every stalk on earth a quill and every man a scribe by trade,
To write the love of God above, would drain the ocean dry.
Nor could the scroll contain the whole, though stretched from
    sky to sky.

—FREDERICK MARTIN LEHMAN, 1868-1953

NEARLY USELESS HANDS

My hands are nearly useless at the foot of Your cross.
They're useless for labor because not a single work
I perform, nor all my works combined could buy
one precious drop of Your forgiveness.

They're useless for bringing things.
   Any offering I could bring looks pale and shabby
      near the reality of Your cross.
         Anything would be an embarrassment.

But maybe these hands aren't entirely useless.

They're good for holding on to You—wrap-
ping my arms around Your cross for dear life.

—JOHN RANDALL DENNIS, 1957-

ROCK OF AGES

—Thomas Hastings, 1830

Rock of A - ges, cleft for me,[1] let me hide my-self in thee;[2]

let the wa - ter and the blood, from thy wound-ed side which flowed,[3]

be of sin the dou-ble cure; save from wrath and make me pure.

2. Not the labor of my hands
   Can fulfill thy law's demands;
   Could my zeal no respite know,
   Could my tears forever flow,
   All for sin could not atone;
   Thou must save, and thou alone.

3. Nothing in my hand I bring,
   Simply to the cross I cling;
   Naked, come to thee for dress;
   Helpless look to thee for grace;[4]
   Foul, I to the fountain fly;
   Wash me, Saviour, or I die.

4. While I draw this fleeting breath,
   When mine eyes shall close in death,
   When I soar to worlds unknown,
   See thee on thy judgment throne,
   Rock of Ages, cleft for me,
   Let me hide myself in thee.[5]

1. 1 Corinthians 10:4
2. Psalm 61:2
3. John 19:34
4. Romans 11:6
5. Isaiah 32:2

—Augustus M. Toplady, 1776

279

ANCIENT OF DAYS

—Jamie Harvill and Gary Sadler, 1992

Bless-ing and ho - nor. Glo-ry and pow - er[1] be un-to the An-cient of Days[2]

From ev - 'ry na - tion all of cre-a - tion bow be-fore the An-cient of Days

Ev - 'ry tongue in heav - en and earth shall de - clare Your glo - ry,

ev - 'ry knee shall bow at Your throne in wor-ship,[3] You will be ex-al-ted O God

Fine

and Your king-dom shall not pass a-way, O An-cient of Days.

Your king-dom shall reign o - ver all the earth. Sing un-to the An-cient of

Days. For none can com - pare to Your match-less worth,

D.C. al Fine

Sing un-to the An - cient of Days.

1. Revelation 5:12
2. Daniel 7:9
3. Philippians 2:10-12

—Jamie Harvill and Gary Sadler, 1992

LIGHTING THE CANDLE

Blessed are you, O Lord our God, King of the Universe, who has sanctified us by His commandments and has commanded us to be a light to nations and has given us Yeshua the Messiah, the Light of the World. Amen.

—EREV SHABBAT BLESSING

SETTLED PEACE

In your occupations, try to possess your soul in peace. It is not a good plan to be in haste to perform any action that it may be sooner over. On the contrary, you should accustom yourself to do whatever you have to do with tranquility, in order that you may retain the possession of yourself and of settled peace.

—MADAME GUYON, 1647–1717

MORNING HAS BROKEN

—TRADITIONAL GAELIC MELODY

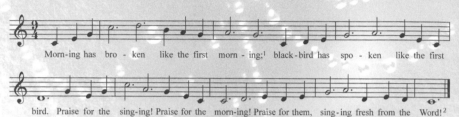

Morn-ing has bro - ken   like the first   morn - ing;[1]   black-bird has   spo - ken   like the first bird.   Praise for the   sing-ing! Praise for the   morn-ing! Praise for them,   sing-ing fresh from the   Word![2]

2. Sweet the rain's new fall, sunlit from heaven,
   Like the first dewfall on the first grass;
   Praise for the sweetness of the wet garden,
   Sprung in completeness where His feet pass.

3. Mine is the sunlight, mine is the morning,
   Born of the One Light Eden saw play;
   Praise with elation, praise every morning,
   God's re-creation of the new day.

1. Genesis 1:5
2. John 1:1-3

—ELEANOR FARJEON, 1931

SIXTEENTH SUNDAY OF THE SEASON AFTER PENTECOST

O Lord, let your continual pity cleanse and defend your Church; and because it cannot continue in safety without you, preserve it evermore by your help and goodness, through Jesus Christ our Lord. Amen.

—THOMAS CRANMER, 1489–1556

BLESSING OVER WIVES

Father, we thank You for giving us wives of Proverbs, and O Lord, I thank you for the wife that You've given me. May you be blessed as you rise while it is yet night to see about the ways of our household and may you be blessed as you see about the daily care and education of our children. May your mouth be filled with wisdom and kindness. May your heart meditate on the power and the glory of the Lord as you do the work of Yeshua. Amen.

—EREV SHABBAT BLESSING

ADORE HIM

The presence of God's glory is in heaven;
the presence of His power on earth;
the presence of His justice in hell;
the presence of His grace with His people.

Fear God for His power.
Trust Him for His wisdom.
Love Him for His goodness.
Praise Him for His greatness.
Believe Him for His faithfulness.
Adore Him for His holiness.

—JOHN MASON, 1646-1694

FAITH

Now *faith,* in the sense in which I am here
using the word, is the art of holding on to
things your reason has once accepted, in
spite of your changing moods.

—C. S. LEWIS, 1898-1963

HOLY, HOLY, HOLY, LORD GOD ALMIGHTY!

—John B. Dykes, 1861

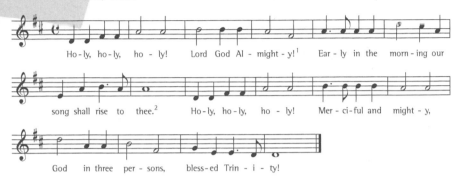

Ho-ly, ho-ly, ho-ly! Lord God Al-might-y![1] Ear-ly in the morn-ing our song shall rise to thee.[2] Ho-ly, ho-ly, ho-ly! Mer-ci-ful and might-y, God in three per-sons, bless-ed Trin-i-ty!

2. Holy, holy, holy! All the saints adore thee,
   Casting down their golden crowns around the glassy sea;[3]
   Cherubim and seraphim falling down before thee,
   Who was, and is, and evermore shall be.[4]

3. Holy, holy, holy! Though the darkness hide thee,
   Though the eye of sinful man Thy glory may not see;
   Only Thou art holy; there is none beside thee,[5]
   Perfect in power, in love, and purity.

4. Holy, holy, holy! Lord God Almighty![6]
   All thy works shall praise thy name, in earth, and sky, and sea;
   Holy, holy, holy; merciful and mighty!
   God in three persons, blessèd Trinity!

1. Revelation 4:8b
2. Psalm 59:16
3. Revelation 4:6
4. Revelation 4:8a
5. 1 Chronicles 17:20
6. Revelation 1:8

—Reginald Heber, 1827

TO HIM WHO SITS ON THE THRONE

—Debbye Graafsma, 1984

To Him who sits on the throne And un-to the Lamb, To Him who

sits on the throne And un-to the Lamb, Be bless-ing and hon-or And

glo - ry and pow-er for - ev - er. Be bless-ing and hon-or And

glo - ry and pow - er for - ev - er. [1]

1. Revelation 5:13

—Debbye Graafsma, 1984

WHEN THE CHURCH MOVES WITH GOD

When the church moves with God, the broken are drawn to God and find healing within the movement.

—ERWIN RAPHAEL MCMANUS, 1958-

BLESSING OVER THE SONS

May the Lord bless you and keep you.
*   May He cause His face to shine upon you.*
May He lift up His countenance and grant you peace.

May you be as Ephraim and Manasseh. May the Lord with you ever be.
May He bring you home unto the land prepared for thee.

May God bless you and grant you long life.

May the Lord fulfill our Sabbath prayer for you.
May God make you good husbands and fathers.

May He prepare a holy wife for you.

May the Lord protect and defend you.
*   May His spirit fill you with grace.*
May our family grow in happiness. O hear our Sabbath prayer. Amen.

—EREV SHABBAT BLESSING

THE NICENE CREED

We believe in one God,
    the Father, the Almighty,
    maker of heaven and earth,
    of all that is, seen and unseen.

We believe in one Lord, Jesus Christ,
    the only Son of God,
    eternally begotten of the Father,
    God from God, Light from Light,
    true God from true God,
    begotten, not made,
    of one Being with the Father.
    Through him all things were made.
    For us and for our salvation he came down from heaven:
by the power of the Holy Spirit he became incarnate from the Virgin Mary,
    and was made man.
For our sake he was crucified under Pontius Pilate;
    he suffered death and was buried.
    On the third day he rose again in accordance with the Scriptures;
    he ascended into heaven and is seated at the right hand of the Father.
He will come again in glory to judge the living and the dead,
    and his kingdom will have no end.

We believe in the Holy Spirit, the Lord, the giver of life,
    who proceeds from the Father and the Son.
    With the Father and the Son he is worshiped and glorified.
    He has spoken through the Prophets.
    We believe in one holy catholic and apostolic Church.
    We acknowledge one baptism for the forgiveness of sins.
    We look for the resurrection of the dead,
        and the life of the world to come. Amen.

SEVENTEENTH SUNDAY OF THE SEASON AFTER PENTECOST

Lord, we pray that your grace may always precede and follow us, and make us continually to be given to all good works, through Jesus Christ our Lord. Amen.

—THOMAS CRANMER, 1489-1556

REVIVAL

Is not the doctrine of the Holy Spirit held slightly? Is he not denied in his person, dishonored in his work, wounded and grieved in his influence? Is there not a more marked dependence on creature power than upon the power of the Spirit? Do not sermons, and books, and reports sadly forget to recognize and honor him as the grand source of all blessing? Are his power, grace, and love, in the great work of conversion, distinctly acknowledged and duly honored?

That there should be no precious gales of grace, no revival of the Lord's work, no true spiritual prosperity where the Holy Spirit is not glorified, we cannot marvel. All must be cold, formal, and lifeless—that church a stagnant pool, and that ministry a powerless instrument, where the Spirit of God is slighted, wounded, or absolutely denied.

—OCTAVIUS WINSLOW, 1808-1878

SUPERLATIVE EXCELLENCE OF THE HOLY SPIRIT

Christ crucified is of no practical value to us without the work of the Holy Spirit; and the atonement which Jesus wrought can never save a single soul unless the blessed Spirit of God shall apply it to the heart and conscience.

—CHARLES SPURGEON, 1834-1892

REVIVE US AGAIN

—JOHN J. HUSBAND, 1815

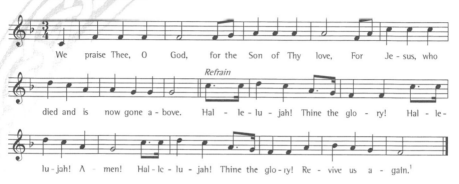

We praise Thee, O God, for the Son of Thy love, For Je-sus, who

Refrain

died and is now gone a-bove. Hal-le-lu-jah! Thine the glo-ry! Hal-le-

lu-jah! A-men! Hal-le-lu-jah! Thine the glo-ry! Re-vive us a-gain.[1]

2. We praise Thee, O God,
   For Thy Spirit of light,
   Who hath shown us our Savior,
   And scattered our night.

   Refrain

3. All glory and praise
   To the Lamb that was slain,[2]
   Who hath borne all our sins,
   And hath cleansed every stain.

   Refrain

4. Revive us again;
   Fill each heart with Thy love;
   May each soul be rekindled
   With fire from above.

   Refrain

1. Psalm 85:6
2. Revelation 5:12

—WILLIAM P. MACKAY, 1863

THOU ART THE KING OF GLORY

Thou art the King of Glory, O Christ.
Thou art the everlasting Son of the Father.

When Thou tookest upon Thee to deliver man,
Thou didst humble Thyself to be born of a virgin.

When Thou hadst overcome the sharpness of death,
Thou didst open the kingdom of heaven to all believers.

Thou sittest at the right hand of God
in the glory of the Father.

We believe that Thou shalt come
to be our judge.

We therefore pray Thee, help Thy servants,
whom Thou hast redeemed with Thy precious blood.

Make them to be numbered with Thy saints
in glory everlasting.

O Lord, save Thy people and bless Thine heritage.
Govern them and lift them up forever.

Day by day we magnify Thee.
And we worship Thy name forever, world without end.

Vouchsafe, O Lord, to keep us this day without sin.
O Lord, have mercy upon us, have mercy upon us.

O Lord, let Thy mercy be upon us, as our trust is in Thee.
O Lord, in Thee have I trusted; let me never be confounded.

—Te Deum Laudamus

TO GOD THE HOLY SPIRIT LET US PRAY

Shine in our hearts, O Spirit, precious light;
Teach us Jesus Christ to know aright
That we may abide in the Lord who bought us,
Till to our true home He has brought us.
Lord, have mercy!

—MARTIN LUTHER, 1483-1546

NOTHING CAN SEPARATE

None of this fazes us because Jesus loves us. I'm absolutely convinced that nothing—nothing living or dead, angelic or demonic, today or tomorrow, high or low, thinkable or unthinkable—absolutely nothing can get between us and God's love because of the way that Jesus our Master has embraced us.

—EUGENE PETERSON, 1932-

(FROM ROMANS 8:37-39 *THE MESSAGE*)

BLESSING OVER THE DAUGHTERS

May the Lord bless you and keep you.
May He cause His face to shine upon you.
May He lift up His countenance and grant you peace.

May you be as Sarah, Rebekah, Rachel, and Leah.
May the Lord with you ever be.
May He bring you home unto the land prepared for thee.

May God bless you and grant you long life.

May the Lord fulfill our Sabbath prayer for you.
May God make you good mothers and wives.

May He bring you a husband who will care for you.

May the Lord protect and defend you.
May His spirit fill you with grace.
May our family grow in happiness. O hear our Sabbath Prayer.

Amen.

—Erev Shabbat Blessing

EIGHTEENTH SUNDAY OF THE SEASON AFTER PENTECOST

Lord, grant your people grace to withstand the temptations of the world, the flesh, and the devil, and with pure hearts and minds to follow you the only God, through Jesus Christ our Lord. Amen.

—THOMAS CRANMER, 1489-1556

CULTIVATE GOD-CONFIDENCE

Don't be so naïve and self-confident. You're not exempt. You could fall flat on your face as easily as anyone else. Forget about self-confidence; it's useless. Cultivate God-confidence.

—EUGENE PETERSON, 1932-

(FROM 1 CORINTHIANS 10:12 *THE MESSAGE*)

CHILDREN OF THE HEAVENLY FATHER

—Swedish Melody

Chil-dren of the heav'n-ly Fa-ther Safe-ly in His bos-om gath-er; Nest-ling bird nor star in heav-en Such a ref-uge e'er was giv-en.

2. God His own doth tend and nourish;
   In His holy courts they flourish;[1]
   From all evil things He spares them;
   In His mighty arms He bears them.

3. Neither life nor death shall ever
   From the Lord His children sever;[2]
   Unto them His grace He showeth,
   And their sorrows all He knoweth.

4. Praise the Lord in joyful numbers:[3]
   Your Protector never slumbers.[4]
   At the will of your Defender
   Ev'ry foeman must surrender.

   1. Psalm 92:13
   2. Romans 8:38-39
   3. Psalm 111:1
   4. Psalm 121:4

—Karolina W. Sandell-Berg, 1858

WE NEED ONLY OBEY

We need only obey. There is guidance for each of us, and by lowly listening we shall hear the right word.

—RALPH WALDO EMERSON, 1803-1882

EXCEED THE NORMAL CAPACITY

When we open ourselves to the Holy Spirit and cease trusting in our own wisdom and power, our actions in accomplishments will far exceed our normal potential and capacity.

—MAXIE DUNNAM, 1934-

AARONIC BLESSING

The Lord bless you and keep you; the Lord make His face shine upon you and be gracious unto you; the Lord lift up His countenance upon you, and give you peace. In the name of Yeshua the Messiah, the Prince of Peace, Shalom.

—EREV SHABBAT BLESSING

OVERCOMING EVIL

If we wish to overcome evil, we must overcome it by good. There are doubtless many ways of overcoming evil in our own hearts, but the simplest, easiest, most universal is to overcome it by active occupation in some good word or work. The best antidote against evil of all kinds, against the evil thoughts which haunt the soul, against the needless perplexities which distract the conscience, is to keep hold of the good we have.

—A. P. STANLEY, 1958–

NINETEENTH SUNDAY OF
THE SEASON AFTER PENTECOST

O God, because without you we are not even able to please you, mercifully grant that your Holy Spirit may in all things direct and rule our hearts, through Jesus Christ our Lord. Amen.

—THOMAS CRANMER, 1489–1556

ENEMY-OCCUPIED TERRITORY

Enemy-occupied territory—that is what this world is. Christianity is the story of how the rightful king has landed, you might say landed in disguise, and is calling us all to take part in a great campaign of sabotage. When you go to church you are really listening-in to the secret wireless from our friends: that is why the enemy is so anxious to prevent us from going.

—C. S. LEWIS, 1898–1963

REJOICE, THE LORD IS KING!

—HARMONIA SACRA, 1753

Re - joice, the Lord is King! Your Lord and King a - dore; mor -
tals, give thanks and sing, and tri - umph ev - er - more. Lift up your
heart, lift up your voice; re - joice; a - gain I say, re - joice.[1]

2. Jesus, the Savior, reigns, the God of truth and love;
   When He had purged our stains He took His seat above;[2]
   Lift up your heart, lift up your voice;
   Rejoice, again I say, rejoice!

3. His kingdom cannot fail, He rules o'er earth and Heav'n,
   The keys of death and hell are to our Jesus giv'n;
   Lift up your heart, lift up your voice;
   Rejoice, again I say, rejoice!

4. He sits at God's right hand till all His foes submit,
   And bow to His command, and fall beneath His feet:[3]
   Lift up your heart, lift up your voice;
   Rejoice, again I say, rejoice!

5. Rejoice in glorious hope! Jesus the Judge shall come,[4]
   And take His servants up to their eternal home.
   We soon shall hear th' archangel's voice;
   The trump of God shall sound, rejoice!

1. Philippians 4:4
2. Colossians 3:1
3. Ephesians 1:22
4. Acts 1:11

—CHARLES WESLEY, 1746

299

GOOD AND FERTILE SOIL

Lord Jesus, make of us good and fertile soil,
for the reception of the seed of your grace,
and make it yield worthy fruits of penance, so
that with your help we may merit to live eternally in
your glory, who are blessed throughout all ages. Amen.

—ANTHONY OF PADUA, 1195-1231

NECESSITY OF THE SPIRIT

The Savior's blood is not more necessary to give you
a title to Heaven than His Spirit to give you a fitness for it.

—JOHN MacDUFF, 1818-1895

OF THE HOLY ANGELS

O everlasting God, who has ordained and constituted the ministries
of angels and men in a wonderful order: Mercifully grant that, as
your holy angels always serve and worship you in heaven, so by
your appointment they may help and defend us on earth, through
Jesus Christ our Lord, who lives and reigns with you and the Spirit,
one God, for ever and ever. Amen.

—THOMAS CRANMER, 1489-1556

LORD, LOOSEN IN ME THE HOLD

Lord, loosen in me the hold of visible things;
Help me to walk by faith and not by sight;
I would, through thickest veils and coverings,
See into the chambers of the living light.
Lord, in the land of things that swell and seem,
Help me to walk by the other light supreme,
Which shows thy facts behind man's vaguely
hinting dream.

—GEORGE MACDONALD, 1824-1905

THIS WORLD IS TOO BARREN

The world is too barren a soil to bear true joy; for where sin within and round about abounds, how can consolation triumph, which rises only as sin falls, and falls as sin rises? But in this my comfort lies— that though in the world I shall have trouble, yet in him I may be of good cheer, because he has overcome the world. Moreover, in the midst of all the sorrow that now surrounds me, I have an inward joy that causes my heart to sing and blossom with the beautiful prospect of eternal joy coming from its divine fountain—which, without the least fear of returning sorrow, shall be the strength of my soul forever!

—JAMES MEIKLE, 1730-1799

TWENTIETH SUNDAY OF THE SEASON AFTER PENTECOST

O Almighty and most merciful God, of your bountiful goodness keep us, from all things that may hurt us; that we, being ready both in body and soul, may cheerfully accomplish those things that you would have done; through Jesus Christ our Lord. Amen.

—THOMAS CRANMER, 1489-1556

I LOOK TO YOU

I close my eyes and look to You. Why am I amazed You smile at me so broadly? You're not who I thought You were at all.

—JOHN RANDALL DENNIS, 1957-

TURN YOUR EYES UPON JESUS

—HELEN H. LEMMEL, 1922

O soul, are you wea-ry and trou - bled? No light in the dark-ness you see?

There's light for a look at the Sav - ior, and life more a - bun-dant and free!

Refrain

Turn your eyes up-on Je - sus, look full in his won-der-ful face

and the things of earth will go strange-ly dim in the light of his glo-ry and grace.[1]

2. Through death into life everlasting[2]
   He passed, and we follow him there;
   Over us sin no more hath dominion—
   For more than conquerors we are!

   Refrain

1. Romans 8:37
2. John 10:10

—HELEN H. LEMMEL, 1922

THE PRODIGAL

His father saw him
   —there were eyes of mercy;
he ran to meet him
   —there were legs of mercy;
he put his arms round his neck
   —there were arms of mercy;
he kissed him
   —there were kisses of mercy;
he said to him
   —there were words of mercy;
Bring here the best robe
   —there were deeds of mercy;

Wonders of mercy
   —all mercy!
Oh, what a God of mercy he is!

—MATTHEW HENRY, 1706-1721

GOD, WHO TOUCHEST EARTH WITH BEAUTY

God, who touchest earth with beauty,
Make me lovely too,
With Thy Spirit recreate me,
Make my life anew.

Like Thy springs of running water
Make me crystal pure.
Like Thy rocks of towering grandeur
Make me strong and sure.
Like Thy dancing waves in sunlight
Make me glad and free.
Like the straightness of the pine-tree
Help me upright be.

Like the arching of Thy heavens,
Raise my thoughts above.
Turn my eyes to noble actions,
Ministries of love.

God, who touchest earth with beauty,
Make me lovely too.
Keep me ever by Thy Spirit,
Pure and strong and true.

—MARY S. EDGAR, 1889-1973

GUIDE ME, O THOU GREAT JEHOVAH

—JOHN HUGHES, 1907

Guide me, O Thou great Je-ho-vah, Pil-grim thro' this bar-ren land. I am weak, but
Thou art might-y;[1] Hold me with Thy pow'r-ful hand. Bread of Heav-en,
Bread of Heav-en, Feed me till I want no more Feed me till I want no more.

2. Open now the crystal fountain,
   Whence the healing stream doth flow;[2]
   Let the fire and cloudy pillar
   Lead me all my journey through.
   Strong Deliverer, strong Deliverer,
   Be Thou still my Strength and Shield;
   Be Thou still my Strength and Shield.[3]

3. When I tread the verge of Jordan,
   Bid my anxious fears subside;
   Death of deaths, and hell's destruction,
   Land me safe on Canaan's side.
   Songs of praises, songs of praises,
   I will ever give to Thee;
   I will ever give to Thee.

1. Psalm 59:9-11
2. Zechariah 13:1
3. Psalm 28:7

—WILLIAM WILLIAMS, 1745

306

LABORERS TOGETHER
WITH GOD

Helpless I am indeed
To right earth's grievous wrong,
To help earth's bitter need
But Thou, my God, art strong.

Too weak I am, I know,
To fight the foes within;
But Thou dost strength bestow
That I may conquer sin.

Naught for life's work have I
But feeble human sense;
Thou dost my need supply
From Thy omnipotence.

Oh, partnership divine,
That thou dost work with me!
What wealth and power are mine!
Since I may work with Thee.

—LUCY ALICE PERKINS, N.D.

TWENTY-FIRST SUNDAY OF
THE SEASON AFTER PENTECOST

Grant to us, merciful Lord, to your faithful people pardon and peace, that we may be cleansed from all our sins and serve you with a quiet mind, through Jesus Christ our Lord. Amen.

—THOMAS CRANMER, 1489–1556

DEEPEST COMMUNION

Deepest communion with God is beyond words,
on the other side of silence.

—MADELEINE L'ENGLE, 1918–

INTIMACY

Intimacy is the deepest cry of the human heart. To be fully known and wholly accepted, to be naked and unashamed. To embrace and be embraced. We could never know this joy but for an accepting and embracing God. Hallelujah! Such is His nature.

—JOHN RANDALL DENNIS, 1957–

GIVE ME YOURSELF, O MY GOD

Give me yourself, O my God, give yourself to me. Behold I love you, and if my love is too weak a thing, grant me to love you more strongly. I cannot measure my love to know how much it falls short of being sufficient, but let my soul hasten to your embrace and never be turned away until it is hidden in the secret shelter of your presence. This only do I know, that it is not good for me when you are not with me, when you are only outside me. I want you in my very self. All the plenty in the world which is not my God is utter want. Amen.

—AUGUSTINE OF HIPPO, 354-430

THE PRESENCE OF GOD

Believe that when you come into the presence of God, you can have all you came for. You can take it away, and you can use it, for all the power of God is at your disposal in response to your faith.

—SMITH WIGGLESWORTH, 1859-1947

ANSWER TO PRAYER

God will do nothing but in answer to prayer.

—JOHN WESLEY, 1703-1791

PRAISE ADONAI

—Paul Baloche, 1999

Who is like Him, The Li-on and the Lamb, seat-ed on the Throne?

Moun-tains bow down, ev'-ry o - cean roars to the Lord of Hosts

Praise A - do - nai from the ri - sing of the sun 'til the

end of ev - 'ry day. Praise A - do - nai all the

na - tions of the earth all the an - gels and the saints sing praise.

—Paul Baloche, 1999

FAITH

Faith sees the invisible, believes the unbelievable, and receives the impossible.

—Corrie ten Boom, 1892-1983

TWENTY-SECOND SUNDAY OF THE SEASON AFTER PENTECOST

Lord, we implore you to keep your household the Church in continual godliness; that through your protection it may be free from all adversities, and devoutly given to serve you in good works, to the glory of your name, through Jesus Christ our Lord. Amen.

—THOMAS CRANMER, 1489-1556

TRUST

Trust the past to the mercy of God,
The present to his love,
The future to his providence.

—AUGUSTINE OF HIPPO, 354-430

INTERCESSION

Let us learn to value the effectual fervent prayers of the righteous. How careful should we be, lest we forfeit our interest in the love and prayers of God's praying people! If we have experienced the Spirit's love, let us not be wanting in this office of kindness for others.

—MATTHEW HENRY, 1706-1721

IN CHRIST

It's in Christ that we find out who we are and what we are living for. Long before we first heard of Christ and got our hopes up, he had his eye on us, had designs on us for glorious living, part of the overall purpose he is working out in everything and everyone.

—EUGENE PETERSON, 1932-

(FROM EPHESIANS 1:11-12 *THE MESSAGE*)

DIALOGUE

Prayer is not monologue, but dialogue. God's voice in response to mine is its most essential part.

—ANDREW MURRAY, 1828-1917

TODAY

Today, Jesus stands ready to hear your cry and to answer prayer for you. He is interested in every detail of your life. He knows you better than you know yourself and is touched with the feeling of your infirmities and your needs.

—KATHRYN KUHLMAN, 1907-1976

YOU HAVE LOVED US FIRST

Father in Heaven! You have loved us first; help us never to forget that You are love so that this sure conviction might triumph in our hearts over the seduction of the world, over the inquietude of the soul, over the anxiety for the future, over the fright of the past, over the distress of the moment.

—Søren Kierkegaard, 1813-1855

TWENTY-THIRD SUNDAY OF THE SEASON AFTER PENTECOST

O God, our refuge and strength, the author of all godliness, be ready to hear the devout prayers of your Church; and grant that those things which we ask faithfully we may obtain effectually, through Jesus Christ our Lord. Amen.

Thomas Cranmer, 1489-1556

REFUGE AND STRENGTH

I know pain or grief does not interrupt your business; but does it not lessen it? You often feel sorrow for your friends; does that sorrow rather quicken than depress your soul? Does it sink you deeper into God? Go on in the strength of the Lord. Be careful for nothing. Live today.

—John Wesley, 1703-1791

O GOD, OUR HELP IN AGES PAST

—WILLIAM CROFT, 1708

O God, our help in a - ges past, our hope for years to come, our

shel - ter from the strom - y blast, and our e - ter - nal Home!¹

2. Under the shadow of Thy
      throne
   Thy saints have dwelt secure;²
   Sufficient is Thine arm alone,
   And our defense is sure.

3. Before the hills in order stood,
   Or earth received her frame,³
   From everlasting Thou art
      God,
   To endless years the same.

4. A thousand ages in Thy sight
   Are like an evening gone;⁴
   Short as the watch that ends
      the night
   Before the rising sun.⁵

5. Time, like an ever rolling
      stream,
   Bears all its sons away;⁶
   They fly, forgotten, as a dream
   Dies at the opening day.

6. O God, our help in ages
      past,
   Our hope for years to come,
   Be Thou our guard while
      troubles last,
   And our eternal home.

1. Psalm 33:20
2. Psalm 90:1
3. Psalm 90:2
4. Psalm 90:4
5. 2 Peter 3:8
6. Psalm 90:10

—ISAAC WATTS, 1719

A HIDDEN POWER

The gospel proclaims a hidden power in the world—
the living presence of the risen Christ.

—BRENNAN MANNING, 1939-

YOU ALONE, LORD

Many are asking, "Who can show us any good?"
Lift up the light of your face on us, O God!
You have put gladness in my heart,
More than when their grain and new wine abound.
In peace I will both lie down and sleep,
For You alone, O Lord, make me to dwell in safety.

—ADAPTED FROM PSALM 4:6-8

I THANK THEE

I thank thee, my heavenly Father, through Jesus
Christ thy dear Son, that thou hast graciously safe-
guarded me this day; and I beseech thee to forgive
me wherein I have erred, and preserve me this night.
I commit my body and soul into thy hands. May thy
holy angel be with me that the wicked one may have
no power over me. Amen.

—MARTIN LUTHER, 1483-1546

O SHOUT AWAY

O Shout, O shout away,
And don't you mind,
And glory, glory, glory in my soul!

And when 'twas night
   I thought 'twas day,
I thought I'd pray my soul away,
And glory, glory, glory in my soul!

O Shout, O shout away,
And don't you mind,
And glory, glory, glory in my soul!

Satan told me not to pray,
He wants my soul at judgment day,
And glory, glory, glory in my soul!

O Shout, O shout away,
And don't you mind,
And glory, glory, glory in my soul!

And everywhere I went to pray,
There some thing was in my way,
And glory, glory, glory in my soul!

—AFRICAN-AMERICAN SPIRITUAL

HELP US

O Father! Help us to resign
Our hearts, our strength, our wills to Thee;
Then even lowliest work of Thine
Most noble, blest, and sweet will be.

—H. M. KIMBALL, n.d.

TWENTY-FOURTH SUNDAY OF
THE SEASON AFTER PENTECOST

O Lord, absolve your people from their offences, that through your bountiful goodness we may all be delivered from the bands of those sins, which by our frailty we have committed: Grant this, O heavenly Father for Jesus Christ's sake, our blessed Lord and Savior. Amen.

—THOMAS CRANMER, 1489-1556

WHITER THAN SNOW

—WILLIAM G. FISCHER, n.d.

Lord Je-sus, I long to be per-fect-ly whole; I want Thee for-ev-er to live in my soul. Break down ev-'ry i-dol; cast out ev-'ry foe. Now wash me and I shall be whit-er than snow.[1]

Refrain

Whit-er than snow, yes, whit-er than snow; Now wash me and I shall be whit-er than snow.

2. Lord Jesus, let nothing unholy remain,
   Apply Thine own blood and extract ev'ry stain;[2]
   To get this blest cleansing, I all things forego—
   Now wash me, and I shall be whiter than snow.

   Refrain

3. Lord Jesus, for this I most humbly entreat,
   I wait, blessèd Lord, at Thy crucified feet.[3]
   By faith, for my cleansing, I see Thy blood flow,
   Now wash me, and I shall be whiter than snow.[4]

   Refrain

4. The blessing by faith, I receive from above;
   O glory! my soul is made perfect in love;[5]
   My prayer has prevailed, and this moment I know,
   The blood is applied, I am whiter than snow.

   Refrain

1. Psalm 51:7
2. Isaiah 1:18
3. Psalm 40:1
4. 1 John 1:7
5. 1 John 4:18

—JAMES NICHOLSON, 1872

THE CROSS

The cross is the emblem of hope; hope constitutes one of its powerful attractions. At the cross, the field of hope is amplified; it is ever opening wider and wider. There is no grief to which it does not furnish mitigation, no evil for which it does not yield an antidote, nor any good which it does not promise.

—GARDINER SPRING, 1785-1873

THE OLD RUGGED CROSS

—GEORGE BENNARD, 1913

On a hill far a-way stood an old rug-ged cross, the em-blem of suf-fering and

shame; and I love that old cross where the dear-est and best for a

Refrain

world of lost sin-ners was slain.[1] So I'll cher-ish the old rug-ged cross, till my

tro-phies at last I lay down I will cling to the old rug-ged cross, and ex-

change it some day for a crown[2]

1. Hebrews 12:2
2. 1 Peter 5:4
3. Hebrews 13:13
4. 2 Timothy 4:8

2. Oh, that old rugged cross, so despised by the world,
Has a wondrous attraction for me;
For the dear Lamb of God left His glory above
To bear it to dark Calvary.
Refrain

3. In that old rugged cross, stained with blood so divine,
A wondrous beauty I see,
For 'twas on that old cross Jesus suffered and died,
To pardon and sanctify me.
Refrain

4. To the old rugged cross I will ever be true;
Its shame and reproach gladly bear;[3]
Then He'll call me some day to my home far away,[4]
Where His glory forever I'll share.
Refrain

—GEORGE BENNARD, 1913

SEEK GOD

How hard it is sometimes to get leave of hearts to seek God! Jesus Christ went more willingly to the cross than we do to the throne of grace.

—THOMAS WATSON, 1637-1717

THIS IS NOT THE PLACE OF DESPAIR

I would say to my soul, O my soul, this is not the place of despair; this is not the time to despair in. As long as mine eyes can find a promise in the Bible, as long as there is a moment left me of breath or life in this world, so long will I wait or look for mercy, so long will I fight against unbelief and despair.

—JOHN BUNYAN, 1628-1688

YIELD

Yield yourself to Christ's claims. Give Him the throne of your heart. Turn over to Him the regulation of your life. Trust in His atoning death. Love Him with all your soul. Obey Him with all your might and He will conduct you to heaven.

—A. W. PINK, 1886-1952

TWENTY–FIFTH SUNDAY OF THE SEASON AFTER PENTECOST

Stir up, O Lord, the wills of your faithful people; that they, plenteously bringing forth the fruit of good works, may by you be plenteously rewarded, through Jesus Christ our Lord. Amen.

—THOMAS CRANMER, 1489–1556

DOXOLOGY

—GENEVAN PSALTER, 1551

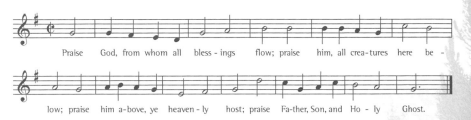

Praise God, from whom all bless - ings flow; praise him, all crea - tures here be - low; praise him a - bove, ye heaven - ly host; praise Fa - ther, Son, and Ho - ly Ghost.

—THOMAS KEN, 1674

Author Index

Song Index

Songs used in *Book of Worship*, LISTED BY SEASON

ADVENT

Come, Thou Long-Expected Jesus 4
O Come, O Come Emmanuel 7
Lo! How a Rose E'er Blooming 10
Let All Mortal Flesh Keep Silence 13
Of the Father's Love Begotten 16
Break Forth, O Beauteous Heavenly Light 21

CHRISTMAS

O Come, All Ye Faithful 26
Silent Night 27
Good Christian Men, Rejoice 28
Angels We Have Heard on High 29
Away in a Manger 31
Hark! the Herald Angels Sing 32
O Little Town of Bethlehem 35
Joy to the World! 37
While Shepherds Watched Their Flocks 38
The First Noel 41

SEASON AFTER PENTECOST